DO-IT-YOURSELF
Projects
FOR Guitarists

35 Useful, Inexpensive Electronic Projects
To Help Unlock Your Instrument's Potential

CRAIG ANDERTON

GPI Books
An Imprint of

Miller Freeman Books

San Francisco

Published by Miller Freeman Books
600 Harrison Street,
San Francisco, CA 94107
Publishers of GPI Books, *Guitar Player, Bass Player* and
Keyboard magazines
A member of the United Newspapers Group

Distributed to the book trade in the U.S. and Canada by
Publishers Group West, P.O. Box 8843, Emeryville, CA 94662

Distributed to the music trade in the U.S. and Canada by
Hal Leonard Publishing, P.O. Box 13819, Milwaukee, WI 53213

Text design and typesetting: Brad Greene
Cover design: Brad Greene
Cover illustration in Photoshop: Jud Guitteau

ISBN 0-87930-359-X

Printed in the United States of America
         98 99   5 4 3 2

CONTENTS

PREFACE

Why bother building your own projects? After all, manufacturers produce a variety of musical goodies at reasonable prices, and lots of musicians get along just fine without ever learning how to solder. But there are still plenty of reasons for rolling up your sleeves and communing with a bunch of parts.

When you build something yourself, chances are you'll know the unit so well that you'll be able to use it to its fullest potential. People who do not understand the principles of how a device operates are often more limited in their ability to apply an effect. Besides, we live in a technological age, and being familiar with electronics can help with much more than just musical devices.

Doing-it-yourself can even become a way of life: it's a short step from building your own guitar gear to keeping your stereo system well-maintained, saving a session when a technical problem crops up, or helping out the neighbor who hasn't figured out how to program a VCR. The idea of taking more control over one's life increases self-respect, which tends to promote confidence in all aspects of life—not just building little boxes.

You'll also find it easier to customize devices for your needs. And if a device messes up, you'll be more inclined to open it up and fix it, saving both time and money. In the process, you'll experience a tremendous amount of personal satisfaction.

Finally, many of the projects in this book have no commercial equivalents. If you want a four-channel fuzz that sounds incredibly clean, a volume pedal de-scratcher, a pickup panpot, or a buffer board that transfers pickup energy to your amp with almost 100% efficiency, you'll have to build it yourself. This can give you a real edge in today's competitive music scene; anything you can do to create a more distinctive and personalized sound is invaluable.

Sure, doing it yourself is not without some frustrations. Sometimes you'll build something and it won't work at first, or maybe a power supply will develop an obnoxious hum the day before the gig, and you'll have to track down the problem.

Eventually, though, you'll fix the problem, and learn a lot during the troubleshooting process ("Gee, so that's what happens when you connect the battery in reverse..."). Then, the moment will come when everything's debugged and working fabulously, you pick up your guitar, and—magic.

Doing it yourself is not always the fastest, easiest, or even the least expensive way of doing things, but it's far and away the most satisfying, educational, and personal. Good luck, and above all, have fun!

Craig Anderton

ACKNOWLEDGMENTS

I'd like to thank the people at *Guitar Player* magazine for giving me the opportunity to write about various guitar projects for over two decades. Many of the devices covered here are based on circuits that first appeared in the pages of *Guitar Player* (along with some from *Keyboard* and *EQ* magazines). Particular thanks go to Joe Gore for saying, "You know, I bet a book of electronic projects based on your columns would go over real well..."

I'd also like to thank Bill Godbout, one of the true pioneers of the personal computer industry, and John Simonton of Paia Electronics, for their encouragement and support over the years. If you took away what I learned from them about electronics, there wouldn't be much left.

Additional thanks go to Mac artist extraordinaire Chuck Dahmer for showing me an alternative to Rapidographs, and to Pat Cameron at Miller Freeman for saying "yes" when I approached her about the idea of doing some books.

Finally, I'd like to thank all the readers who have given me so much support in my endeavors. Your cards and letters, and the occasional in-person meeting, have enriched my life more than you could ever know. You're the reason why I write these books...so I hope you like this one. Thanks again!

How to Read Schematics

If you ever want to rewire a guitar or build one of the nifty gadgets in this book, you need to know how to read schematics. Luckily, it isn't all that hard, and you'll gain a lot. Having a bit of electronic know-how can really save the day when you have to repair a cord, find out why your guitar isn't working, or make some little box that will simplify your life.

Writing out a schematic is conceptually no different from writing out music notation: a set of standardized symbols allow you to communicate your thoughts with others who understand the meaning of these symbols. Also like music notation, some people are great sight readers—they can spend a few seconds looking at a schematic, and know exactly what's going on in a given circuit. Others have to spend some time "deciphering" the schematic until it makes sense. Either way, though, the meaning gets communicated.

Simply stated, schematics are wiring diagrams that require little, if any, artistic talent. Even the simplest circuit could take hours to complete if you had to draw every little resistor, solder connection, and wire. Surely there's an easier way to do things, and that's where the schematic comes in.

By using symbols that correspond to electronic components, the process of defining a circuit becomes much easier. So, let's look at some of the common schematic symbols, and how they relate to "real-world" parts.

A SIMPLE CIRCUIT

Suppose you want to show someone how to wire up a single pickup to a tone control, volume control, and output jack. Fig. 1-1 is my attempt at doing a freehand wiring diagram using a mouse (don't laugh, please). While this may seem clear, even with a circuit this simple there could be some confusing points. For example, the output jack is kind of hard to draw, and you might be confused about which jack terminal is supposed to go to which wire. Now let's turn this wiring diagram into a schematic.

Fig. 1-1
Hand drawn wiring diagram.

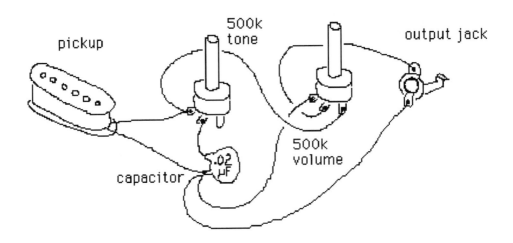

WIRING

Since we have a bunch of wires draped all over the place, we need a symbol for wire (see Fig. 1-2). There's certainly nothing difficult to understand about this symbol.

Fig. 1-2
Symbol for wire.

If we want to show that a wire connects to another wire, draw a little dot at the intersection (Fig. 1-3).

Fig. 1-3
Wire connecting to another wire.

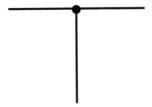

The circuit also uses two potentiometers (controls), so we need a symbol for those. To understand this symbol, we need to understand how a potentiometer works. Essentially, a potentiometer is a variable resistor. A resistor is a device that resists the flow of current, which is exactly what you want to do when you turn down a volume control.

RESISTORS

Fig. 1-4 shows the schematic symbol for a resistor, along with what a real-world resistor looks like. Notice that representing the resistor with a zig-zag line actually tells you a bit about what the part does; after all, if you were an electron wouldn't you slow down a little bit going through all those hairpin turns?

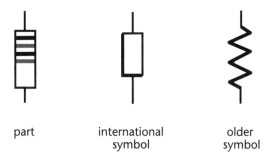

part   international symbol   older symbol

Fig. 1-4
A resistor along with two associated schematic symbols.

The unit of resistance is the *ohm,* abbreviated as Ω. In other words, 470 ohms = 470Ω. An ohm is a relatively small unit of resistance, so you'll often see resistor values given in kilohms (1,000 ohms, abbreviated k) and megohms (1,000,000 ohms, abbreviated M). For example, a 47,000Ω resistor will be shown as a 47kΩ, or simply 47k, resistor.

INTERNATIONAL VS. AMERICAN RESISTOR VALUES

American schematics abbreviate resistor values a little differently from European schematics and schematics from most parts of the world. In international schematics when a resistor value includes a decimal point *(i.e.,* 4.7k, 2.2M), the k or M inserts where the decimal point would normally appear. This helps reduce the chance of typos, which is why the schematics in this book give the resistor values in international nomenclature (the parts list gives the American values as well). Here are some examples of American nomenclature and the international equivalents:

American	International
1.8k	1k8
5.6k	5k6
1.2M	1M2
4.7M	4M7

If there is no decimal point in the resistor value, then the metric and American designations are the same.

POTENTIOMETERS

What makes a *potentiometer* different from a resistor is a third terminal that allows you to tap anywhere along the resistance. Incorporating the third terminal into our diagram provides the symbol for a potentiometer (Fig. 1-5). The little arrow indicates that the third terminal, also called the *wiper,* doesn't connect directly to the resistor, but can actually "point" to any place along the resistor. So again, once you know what to look for, the symbol tells you something about the function of the part that it represents.

Fig. 1-5
Symbols for a poten-
tiometer.

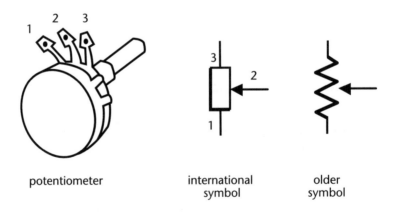

potentiometer   international symbol   older symbol

Like resistors, potentiometer values are given in ohms. Also note that the potentiometer has its terminals numbered. These correspond to numbers on the schematics in this book that indicate which wires go to which potentiometer terminals. When viewed from the front, turning a potentiometer fully clockwise connects terminal 2 to terminal 3; fully counterclockwise connects terminal 2 to terminal 1.

There's also a variation on the potentiometer, called a *trimpot*. These are small potentiometers that aren't designed for continuous use, but for set-and-forget applications—you set them to the position you want and leave them that way. They're usually mounted internally to a piece of gear, although sometimes there will be an access hole drilled in the case so you can adjust the trimpot with a small screwdriver.

CAPACITORS

Fig. 1-6
Capacitor symbol.

We still have three parts that need symbols: the 0.02 µF capacitor, the pickup, and the jack. Since a capacitor is technically just a couple of plates separated by an insulator and put in a package, our symbol (Fig. 1-6) symbolically shows the two plates separated by an insulator. Whenever you see this symbol, you know you're dealing with a capacitor. We'll talk more about capacitor types and values later on in this chapter.

PICKUPS

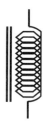

Fig. 1-7
Pickup symbol.

A pickup is just a bunch of turns of wire around a metal bar; in Fig. 1-7, you can see the metal bar represented by straight lines, and the coil of wire represented by—well, something that looks like a coil of wire.

JACKS

Fig. 1-8
Symbol for a mono, open circuit phone jack.

This leaves us with the jack (Fig. 1-8). Again, you'll notice a close resemblance to a side view of the real-world part, down to the little contact that mates with the matching plug to make a firm connection.

A SIMPLE CIRCUIT, REVISITED

Fig. 1-9 shows the equivalent of Fig. 1-1, but this time in schematic form. Note how this is much easier to draw, less confusing (once you know what the symbols stand for, of course), and is standardized so that anybody conversant in schematics can look at this diagram and know what's going on.

This is a very basic circuit, but it should get the idea across about schematics. Now let's dig a little deeper.

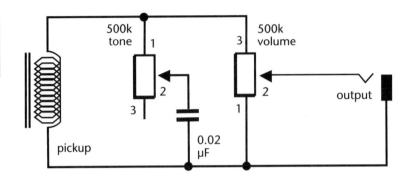

**Fig. 1-9
The completed
schematic.**

CAPACITORS

The capacitor symbol in Fig. 1-6 is a *non-polarized* capacitor, meaning that the two leads are interchangeable. In other words, if there are two holes in a circuit board for a capacitor, either lead can go in either hole.

A battery is an example of a *polarized* part, since each lead is different *(e.g.,* one is positive, the other negative). With a polarized part, it's important to note which lead is which. The most common polarized capacitors are called *electrolytic* or *tantalum* capacitors; these names refer to the material used to make the capacitors. Just like a battery, electrolytic and tantalum capacitors have plus (+) and minus (-) leads, which must be hooked up correctly for the circuit to work. If the (+) lead is marked, then the other lead is (-) and vice-versa.

Fig. 1-10 shows two types of electrolytic capacitor (axial, where the leads come out opposite ends; and radial, where the

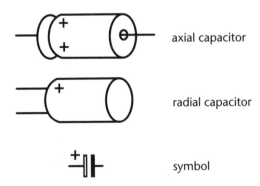

**Fig. 1-10
Axial and radial ca-
pacitors, with their
schematic symbol.**

axial capacitor

radial capacitor

symbol

DO-IT-YOURSELF PROJECTS FOR GUITARISTS

leads come out the same end) along with the associated schematic symbol. To indicate polarity, the schematic symbol includes a little (+) sign in the vicinity of the positive plate (sometimes there will be a minus sign as well).

The unit of capacitance is the *farad,* but this is an extremely large amount of capacitance. Therefore, capacitor values are given in microfarads (1/1,000,000th of a farad), abbreviated as μF, and in picofarads (1/1,000,000,000,000th of a farad), abbreviated as pF.

INTERNATIONAL VS. AMERICAN CAPACITOR VALUES

Like resistors, capacitor values are also shown differently on American schematics compared to the rest of the world. In addition to the μF and pF, international schematics frequently use the term nanofarad (abbreviated nF), which equals 0.000000001 farads. Here are common capacitor values expressed in μF, pF, and nF:

0.001μF =	1,000pF =	1nF
0.01μF =	10,000pF =	10nF
0.1μF =	100,000pF =	100nF

When a capacitor value includes a decimal point (*i.e.,* 2.2μF, 3.9pF, 5.6nF), the μ, p, or n goes where the decimal point would normally appear. Here are some examples of American nomenclature and the international equivalents:

American	International
3900pF	3n9
2.2μF	2μ2
0.1μF	100nF
5.6pF	5p6

It generally takes fewer characters to write the international value, and there's no chance of putting a decimal point in the wrong place because there is no decimal point. As with resistors, the schematics in this book show capacitor values in international nomenclature (the parts list gives American values also).

DIODES AND LEDS

Like electrolytic capacitors, these are also polarized components. The diode is somewhat like an electronic switch, while the LED (light-emitting diode) generates light when you hit it with a couple of volts. Fig. 1-11 shows a diode, along with its schematic symbol. Note that the diode has a little painted band going around it, which is closer to one end of the part than the other. This band marks the *cathode,* or negative, end of the

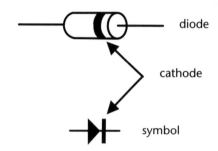

Fig. 1-11
A diode and its asso-
ciated symbol.

diode. In the schematic symbol, the diode's arrow points toward the cathode. So, if you see a schematic with a diode symbol, make sure you orient the diode's cathode as shown on the schematic.

The LED symbol (Fig. 1-12) is similar to the diode, except for a little circle around the diode and some arrows to represent light shooting out of the LED. The way to identify an LED's cathode lead is either from a little painted dot or flat spot in the case next to the appropriate lead. The upper part of Fig. 1-12 shows how the flat spot identifies the cathode.

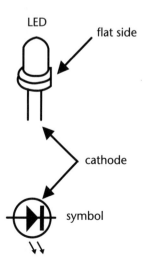

Fig. 1-12
LED and its symbol.
The flat side of the
case indicates the
cathode.

BIPOLAR TRANSISTORS

Transistors are also polarized but now we're dealing with a
three-terminal, not two-terminal, device. A transistor's three
leads are called the *emitter* (where electrons are "emitted"), the
collector (which "collects" these emitted electrons), and the *base*
(which regulates the amount of conduction between the emitter and collector terminals).

There are also two different families of bipolar transistors,
NPN and PNP. You don't need to know the theory behind PNP
vs. NPN, but you do need to recognize the difference between
their schematic symbols. Fig. 1-13 shows the schematic symbol
for an NPN transistor along with the PNP equivalent. The only
difference is the direction of the emitter arrows.

Fig. 1-13
NPN and PNP transis-
tor symbols.

To relate the symbol to the part, many plastic packaged
transistors will have little E, C, and B letters embossed next to
the emitter, collector, and base leads. However, not all transistors have these embossed letters, and unfortunately, not all
transistors follow a standard lead layout. Fig. 1-14 identifies the
two most common transistor lead layouts (note that these are
bottom views of the transistors). Data books describing the part
are the ultimate authority for which lead is which.

Fig. 1-14
Two popular types of
transistor case styles
(bottom view).

POWER AND GROUND

Many circuits use a *bipolar* supply (which provides both positive and negative voltages), while other circuits simply use a single positive or negative supply. In the schematics in this book, a circled (-) symbol means connect that point to the negative supply point, and a circled (+) symbol means connect that point to the positive supply point.

Another way of indicating power supply connections (not used in this book) is with arrows. An arrow pointing up connects to the positive supply, and an arrow pointing down connects to the negative supply.

Grounding is a subject that could take up half this book. Ideally, all points with a ground symbol (see Fig. 1-15) should connect through their own piece of wire to the power supply ground. In most cases this would require too many wires, so the builder must know enough to decide which points can be connected together and then connected to ground, and which points must have their own lead to ground. As a rule of thumb, you can assume that ground wires carrying a significant amount of current, or ground wires that connect to high gain circuitry, should have individual ground return wires.

**Fig. 1-15
Power supply symbols.**

connects
to ground

connects to
positive
power supply

connects to
negative
power supply

INTEGRATED CIRCUITS

The most common audio analog integrated circuit is the op amp, which is a type of amplifier and looks like a block of epoxy with pins sticking out of it. Viewed from above, the IC (integrated circuit) will have a dot next to pin 1, or a notch to the right of pin 1. To figure out the pin numbering, locate pin 1; the next pin down is 2, 3, 4, and so on. You then jump over to the other side of the IC, and start counting *up* from there. Fig. 1-16

DO-IT-YOURSELF PROJECTS FOR GUITARISTS

shows the pin numbering scheme and pinouts (*i.e.,* what each pin represents) for several of the ICs used in this book. Keep reading for more information about pinouts.

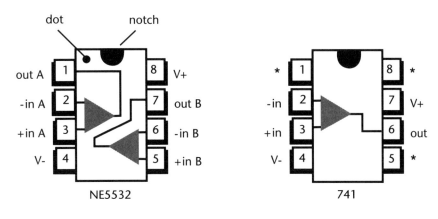

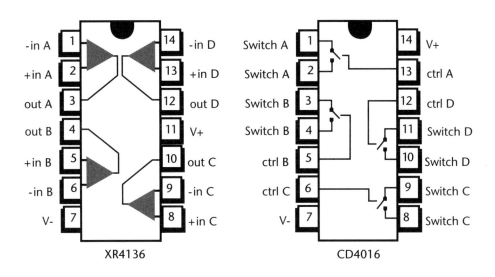

Fig. 1-17 shows the schematic symbol for a typical op amp. There are two inputs (inverting and non-inverting), one output, and two power supply leads (+ is positive, - is negative). Written inside the op amp is the generic identifying number (in this case, 741) or if part of a schematic, an identification such as IC1. Next to each lead is a number that corresponds to the pin number of the IC. In the example shown, pin 2 is the inverting input, pin 7 the positive power supply line, and so on. To wire up an op amp, you simply match the pin numbers on

> **Fig. 1-16**
> **Numbering for 8-pin and 14-pin IC cases and pinouts for four integrated circuits.**

the schematic to the pins on the actual IC, as shown on the pinout.

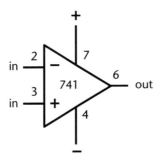

Fig. 1-17
Schematic symbol
for a 741 op amp.

Some schematics don't show pin numbers for op amps, while others don't show power supply connections. These schematics assume that the builder knows enough to choose an appropriate op amp and knows, or can look up, the most popular pin configurations. This practice is not just done to confuse beginners; there is a legitimate reason. Suppose a project requires four op amps. As it happens, sometimes op amps are packaged two to a single 8 pin IC (dual op amp) or even four to a single 14 pin IC (quad op amp). So, depending on what parts you had on hand, and assuming that the op amps can substitute for each other, you could build the circuit using one quad op amp, two dual op amps, or four single op amps. Also, not all op amps follow consistent power or signal connections; pin 2 might be the (-) input for one op amp, and the output for another type.

To determine which pin is which, it's necessary to determine the part's pinout by looking in the manufacturer's data book or checking any data included with the IC. For example, Radio Shack semiconductors often include the pinout on the back of the package, along with some minimal electronic information about the part.

Data books are wonderful sources of information, but are costly and sometimes difficult to find. In most cases, data included with the part should tell you which pin is which. Incidentally, any pin not shown on a schematic should generally be ignored; don't connect it to anything. If there are exceptions to this rule, it should be noted in the text accompanying the

DO-IT-YOURSELF PROJECTS FOR GUITARISTS

schematic (such as "all unused pins connect to ground," or whatever).

Some ICs do not have a standard symbol. In this case, we simply draw a rectangle and put pin numbers next to the leads (see Fig. 1-18). As long as you can correctly identify the IC pins, you'll be in good shape. Remember, though, if you don't see any power supply connections, read the accompanying text carefully to see if there are additional instructions concerning power or ground connections.

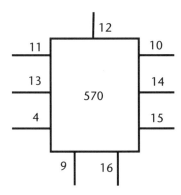

Fig. 1-18
Schematic symbol for one section of a 570 IC, which contains two independent sections.

BATTERIES

Batteries are easy (see Fig. 1-19): the (+) terminal is a long line, and the (-) terminal is a shorter line. In addition, you'll see a polarity mark to make things even clearer, just like a capacitor. You'll also see a number indicating the voltage. With 9V transistor radio battery connectors, the red lead indicates the battery's (+) terminal, and the black lead indicates the battery's (-) terminal.

Fig. 1-19
Battery symbol.

TRANSFORMERS

When you're not using batteries, you'll be dealing with AC power supplies, and they require transformers. If Fig. 1-20 reminds you of the pickup symbol shown in Fig. 1-7, that's because a transformer also uses coils. The coil that connects to 117 VAC is

primary   secondary

Fig. 1-20
Center-tapped transformer symbol.

called the *primary,* and the coil that connects to the rest of the power supply is the *secondary* (in this case, it's a *center-tapped secondary*). Usually the primary leads will be black and white or both black, while the secondary leads will be more colorful.

The center tap is a feature of some transformers, and lets you treat the unit as having two secondaries instead of one. For example, a transformer with a 12V center-tapped secondary can be treated as having two 6 VAC secondaries.

SWITCHES

Fig. 1-21 shows the schematic symbol for a single pole, single throw (SPST) switch; closing the switch completes the circuit. A *pole* is the lead to be switched, and the *throw,* the lead to which it can be switched. For example, a single pole, double throw switch (SPDT) can switch one lead to your choice of two other leads.

Fig. 1-21
Single pole, single
throw (SPST) switch.

Fig. 1-22 shows a double pole, double throw (DPDT) switch, along with what the bottom of such a switch looks like. The DPDT switch simultaneously switches each pole to one of two other leads per pole. Note how the pin arrangement on the DPDT switch exactly resembles the schematic symbol. If you're not sure which terminals connect together for different switch positions, you can always trace it through using a VOM (volt-ohm-milliameter), multimeter, or continuity tester.

Fig. 1-22
DPDT switch symbol,
and the bottom of
a DPDT switch case.
The two center
terminals are the
two poles.

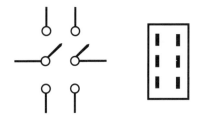

Fig. 1-23 shows a rotary switch, where one pole connects to any one of 6 positions. Usually, a close look at the switch will

DO-IT-YOURSELF PROJECTS FOR GUITARISTS

reveal which terminal on the part corresponds to which connection on the schematic; you'll actually see a piece of metal that connects to the "pole" wiping across a number of different contacts (the "throws"). Note that you can use a 1P6T rotary switch as a 1P5T, 1P4T, or 1P3T simply by ignoring some of the switch terminals.

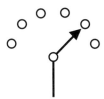

Fig. 1-23
Rotary switch sche-
matic for a single
pole, six-throw type.

That's enough about schematics for now; hopefully you've gotten the idea at this point and are ready to start building.

Construction Basics

Proper construction can make the difference between a working circuit and a useless pile of parts. A complete description of how to build electronic devices from scratch is beyond the scope of this book, which is intended more as a collection of projects for those who are already familiar with electronics; but we'll at least cover the basics.

If you're a novice, I suggest checking out my book *Electronic Projects for Musicians* (published by AMSCO), which gives detailed information on electronic construction techniques. I also recommend *How to Service Your Own Tube Amp,* a book/video program by Tom Mitchell. The book is well done and covers lots of basic electronic and electrical concepts; the video is for those situations where a picture is worth a thousand words.

Also note that several of these projects are commercially available in kit form from Paia Electronics. For details, see the end of this chapter.

TOOLS

The most important tools you need are:

- Variable speed electric drill with a selection of bits 1/16", 1/8", and 3/8" are particularly important). *Be careful when drilling!*

Always hold the object to be drilled in a vise, not with your hands. Also, don't wear any jewelry while drilling, and make sure to keep your hair out of the way of the bit. Keep drill bits perpendicular to the object being drilled to avoid snapping them in two.

- Center punch to create a small indentation prior to drilling.

- Fine-toothed hacksaw for cutting potentiometer shafts to the desired length.

- Small, adjustable crescent wrench for tightening nuts on pots and screws.

- Small rat's tail file and half-round file to clean up drilled holes and cut potentiometer shafts.

- Needlenose pliers for bending and working with wire and component leads. Get a small pliers and use it only for light work; if you need something heavier-duty, get a vise grips.

- Diagonal cutters for cutting wire and component leads.

- Wire stripper for removing insulation from hookup wire.

- An assortment of screwdrivers, including Phillips head and jeweler's types as well as regular flat types. Make sure the screwdriver fits tightly into the screw's slot, or you'll damage both the screw and screwdriver.

- A small vise to hold parts for soldering, sawing, or filing.

- 40 watt to 60 watt, small-tipped soldering pencil or (for those who like to go first class) a temperature-controlled soldering station. Wear eye protection while soldering; sometimes the rosin can spit out. Also, solder in a well-ventilated area.

- 60/40 rosin-core "multicore" solder intended specifically for electronics work. Never, under any circumstances, use acid core solder—this is intended for plumbing and will destroy your circuit (really!).

- Squeeze bulb or other desoldering tool for when you need to remove something.

- Ground strap for installing ICs in their sockets. Some ICs are static-sensitive, and a ground strap discharges static electricity from you during the installation process.

THE BUILDING PROCESS

Most projects follow the same basic steps:

1. Gather the parts together. Some of these projects are available as kits, which greatly simplifies the parts-gathering process. Aside from that, large metropolitan areas often have electronic parts distributors (try the Yellow Pages under "Electronic Equipment and Supplies—Dealers" and "Electronic Equipment and Supplies—Wholesale"). However, the best alternative is usually mail order. Go to your local newsstand and buy some copies of magazines for electronic hobbyists (such as *Popular Electronics, Audio Amateur,* and *Electronics Now).* Their back pages are filled with ads from mail order suppliers. Send away for catalogs and you'll have access to some great parts sources.

2. Mount the components on a circuit board and solder them in place. Proper soldering technique is crucial! The surfaces to be soldered must be clean and free of oxidation; use steel wool if necessary to clean metal surfaces. Also, always heat the area to be soldered for a few seconds before feeding in the solder. Feed in just enough solder to make a strong connection, not a big blob, and let it flow freely over the joint. Withdraw the iron tip and make sure you don't move the connection as it cools; if so, you'll need to reheat it.

Regarding circuit boards, the best option for experimenters is to use perf board and flea clips. Perf board is a phenolic board with holes on (usually) $\frac{1}{10}$" centers. You poke components through the holes, and wire them together. The flea clips are small clips that insert in the holes and serve as "anchors" for larger parts, or for wires that go to outboard components.

Printed circuit boards are a real art form and are difficult to make for the novice. However, many electronics stores sell kits for making your own boards, and boards for some of these projects are available from Paia Electronics.

You'll generally mount resistors and sockets first, followed by capacitors, diodes, LEDs, then any remaining parts. Remember to check the polarity of polarized parts, and for proper solder connections. I'd recommend using sockets for ICs, as this simplifies repair and prevents heat damage from soldering.

3. Select an enclosure. Small aluminum boxes and rack panels are ideal. Always use aluminum instead of steel, which is very difficult to work with. Plastic boxes are acceptable in some cases, but are not as sturdy and require special drill bits for drilling large holes. The lack of shielding can also be a problem.

4. Drill holes in the enclosure for the various "outboard" components (controls, switches, etc.). The easiest way to do this is to get some graph paper and draw a template. Once you're satisfied that all the components will fit, use the center punch to mark each hole, then drill a small pilot hole. Enlarge the hole if necessary with a larger bit after drilling the pilot hole.

If you have a variable speed drill, start at a slow speed to make sure the drill bit is centered, then increase the speed.

5. Mount the circuit board in the enclosure and wire the outboard components to the circuit board. Use stranded, not solid, wire as it's more flexible. Your best bet is insulated hookup wire in the range of #24 to #26 gauge (this is a measure of the wire's thickness; you don't want it too thick or too thin). When removing insulation, be careful not to nick the wire. Also, don't remove too much insulation, or the wire may short out to other components.

To mount the circuit board, either use long screws and spacers or small metal brackets. Make sure the circuit board can't loosen over time, or it may short out to the enclosure and cause problems.

6. Add labels and knobs.

7. Test the completed circuit. Look over your work one last time, paying particular attention to the orientation of polarized parts, and the quality of the solder connections. After applying power, check for acrid smells, smoke, or other signs of problems. If something seems wrong, shut off power immediately and trace the source of the problem.

TROUBLESHOOTING PROJECTS

It's rare that a project works perfectly the first time (if it does, congratulate yourself!). Usually there will be some little bug, like a control wired in reverse, or a missed connection. Most problems are due to human error, such as an IC inserted backwards or cold solder joint. Also remember that most devices have a learning curve, and it may take a little while to figure out how to get the most out of a project. For example, the more flexibility a project offers, the longer it takes to find the optimum control settings to get "your" sound.

Although the projects in this book aren't too difficult, human error is always a factor. At that point, it's time to get into troubleshooting and debugging mode. Although it's impossible to get too specific—each problem has its own unique solution—here are some general guidelines that will hopefully make the troubleshooting process a little easier.

- Realize that you are going to make errors. Most beginners are crushed when they find out that their problem is due to some "stupid" mistake, such as a bad solder connection or IC inserted backwards. Relax—experts make these mistakes too; the only difference is that experts aren't as inconvenienced by mistakes, because they can track the error down much faster than someone who has had less experience.

- Break troubleshooting down into the smallest possible chunks. For example, suppose you build the "Clarifier" preamp. First see what does work; if the treble boost works but the bass boost doesn't, then you know the problem has something to do with the bass control or its associated circuitry.

  If the circuit doesn't seem to work right at all, check those elements which are common to the entire circuit, such as the power supply. Many times the only thing standing between a successful project and a pile of parts is a missing ground line or power supply lead.

- Look for the obvious. Misset controls, ICs inserted backwards, dead batteries—these kinds of things happen all the time. Some people get so hung up on checking capacitor polarity and diodes they fail to notice an IC with a pin sticking out of its socket or a bad solder joint.

- Suspect mechanical problems first. This includes bad solder joints, one of the major causes of problems (sometimes just re-heating all your solder joints is sufficient to fix the problem). Also be on the lookout for cracked resistors, parts with internal shorts (measure them with an ohmmeter), broken switches, and the like.

- Make sure your peripheral equipment is in good shape. Someone wrote me once saying that his project had an intermittent problem (it produced crackling sounds in his amp), and did I have any suggestions. I told him to check his guitar cord, and write back if the problem persisted. He never wrote back.

- Oscilloscopes are wonderful tools. An oscilloscope provides a pictorial representation of what's happening in a circuit, so you can compare something like the signal going into a preamp and what comes out of it. Oscilloscopes will also teach you a lot about audio, and are extremely valuable if you ever get into recording. You don't need an expensive oscilloscope for audio troubleshooting; a simple second-hand unit (check garage sales) will do the job just fine.

Finally, and perhaps most importantly, make sure the cure isn't worse than the disease. Once I was testing a circuit for a fairly minor problem, but then the test probe slipped, shorted out the power supply, and created a complicated (and expensive!) problem. Then there was the time that I was fixing a friend's delay line that had a nasty oscillation. I soldered in a bypass capacitor to try to kill the oscillation, but that only made things worse. Eventually, I found that the regeneration and output controls had been reversed, so when I thought I was turning up the output, I was really turning up the regeneration, and that's what was producing the oscillation.

But that wasn't the end of it. After an afternoon of frustration, I eventually figured out that the bypass capacitor I added way back in the beginning had a lead going to the wrong pin on an IC! So, my attempts to fix the thing actually created more of a problem.

Moral of the story: label your controls correctly, and yes, troubleshooting can sometimes turn into a wild goose chase if you overlook the obvious problems and look instead for sophisticated little bugs.

PARTS KITS

By special arrangement with Paia Electronics, several of the projects in this book are available in kit form. Some individual components, such as integrated circuits, printed circuit boards, and front panels are also available. Since pricing and availability are subject to change, contact Paia for their latest catalog with information on these projects:

Paia Electronics, 3200 Teakwood Lane, Edmond, OK 73013. Tel. (405) 340-6300.

One-Evening Projects

✳ PROJECT 1
WALL WART TAMER

Wall transformers for gear can cut down on hum and simplify UL approval, but because of their size, they generally use up more than one receptacle on a barrier strip. Also, leaving them plugged in when no current is being drawn can shorten the transformer's life. Here's a simple project that will reclaim some barrier strip outlets, as well as let you turn off power independently of the barrier strip switch.

The wall wart tamer (Fig. 3-1) consists of a one- to two-foot length of two-conductor zip cord, and three parts that can attach to zip cord without any soldering: AC receptacle (GE

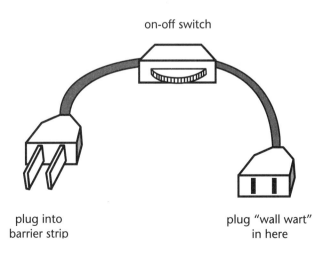

on-off switch

plug into
barrier strip

plug "wall wart"
in here

> **Fig. 3-1**
> **The utterly simple Wall Wart Tamer wiring diagram. If you can't build this, don't even think about a career in electronics.**

Quick Clamp Connector, part #GE1710-21D, or equivalent), on-off switch (ACE Hardware Quick Connect Cord Switch, part #ACE 31089, or equivalent), and plug (ACE Hardware Quick Connect Plug, part #ACE 31099 or equivalent). Clip the receptacle and plug to opposite ends of the zip cord, and the switch in between (Fig. 3-1). Plug the transformer into the receptacle, and the plug into your barrier strip. Use the switch to turn off the AC when the unit isn't in use.

Simple, eh?

✱ PROJECT 2
AC ADAPTER HUM BUSTER

If hum from an AC adapter is messing up your sound, this extremely simple circuit could solve your problem once and for all.

The AC adapters (wall transformers) that come with commercial gear are optimized for what they're powering. However, if you use an off-the-shelf AC adapter from a local electronics store, either as a replacement for an adapter that broke or to power do-it-yourself projects, you may be disappointed. Many adapters do not produce well-filtered DC, which is acceptable for powering something like a calculator (you won't hear any "dirt" in the power supply anyway) but may produce ugly hum when hooked up to your audio-related project.

Fig. 3-2
The upper diagram is for positive tip AC adapters, and the lower diagram for negative tip models.

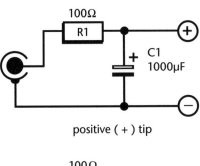

positive (+) tip

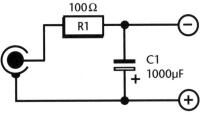

negative (-) tip

Fig. 3-2 shows a solution that works in almost all cases. The upper diagram shows a circuit for AC adapters with positive tip plugs; the lower diagram works with adapters with negative tip plugs (a label on the adapter's body will usually indicate the type).

R1 and C1 provide additional filtering to convert the "raw" DC into a cleaner, purer voltage. To be conservative, C1's working voltage should be rated at twice the adapter's output voltage (*e.g.,* for a 6V adapter, use a 12V capacitor).

Regarding construction, many times you can simply mount these two components in the piece of equipment being powered to save yourself the hassle of constructing a box.

PARTS LIST

R1	100 Ω resistor
C1	1000 µF capacitor (see text for working voltage)

* PROJECT 3
MAKING CROSSFADE AND PANPOT PEDALS

A conventional stereo volume pedal can do a lot more than just regulate volume. With a little rewiring, you can turn it into a crossfade pedal that fades between two inputs and sends the result to a single output, or a panpot pedal, which pans a single input to left and right outputs.

A stereo volume pedal consists of two inputs, two outputs, and two potentiometers that regulate the level between the ins

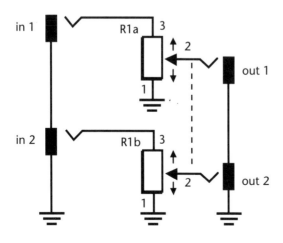

Fig. 3-3
Schematic for a typical stereo volume pedal.

and outs. Fig. 3-3 shows the wiring for a typical stereo pedal; R1 is a *dual ganged* potentiometer (*i.e.*, two separate potentiometers are connected together mechanically) so that turning down one control also turns down the other control.

CROSSFADE PEDAL MODIFICATION

Fig. 3-4 shows how to modify this to create a crossfade pedal. The main differences are that input 1 now connects to what used to be R1a's ground terminal, and R1a's hot terminal now connects to ground. As R1a turns up input 1's volume, R1b turns down input 2's volume, and vice-versa. This provides the crossfading action between the two inputs.

The middle terminal for both controls connect together and feed an output (in this case, they're both wired to output 2). If desired, you could connect output 1 in parallel with output 2 so that you have two paralleled output jacks.

Fig. 3-4
How to modify a stereo volume pedal to create a crossfade pedal.

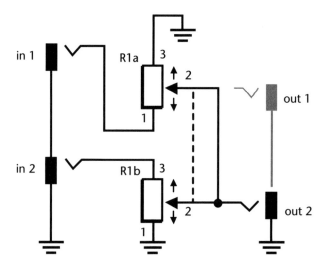

PANPOT PEDAL MODIFICATION

Fig. 3-5 shows the panpot pedal modification, which is similar to the crossfade pedal since R1a's hot and ground terminals are again reversed. However, input 2 feeds both R1a and R1b, which retain their separate outputs. As R1a increases the level going to the left output, R1b decreases the level going to the right output. This creates the panning effect.

One option is to parallel input 1 and input 2, so that for convenience's sake you could plug into either input.

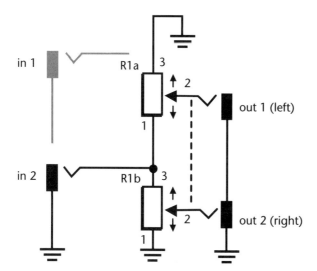

in 1   R1a   3

2   out 1 (left)

1

in 2   R1b   3

2   out 2 (right)

1

✳ PROJECT 4
EFFECTS ORDER SWITCHER

Here's an easy way to eliminate switching patch cords around when you want to reverse the order of a pair of effects—just flick a switch.

With series effects systems (see the Buffer Board project, for a description of series effects), the order in which effects occur can make a huge difference to the overall sound. For example, distortion before equalization sounds vastly different compared to equalization before distortion.

Although you can patch cables around to try out different orders of effects, that can be tedious—and for on-stage use, you'd certainly want a more convenient option. The following circuit is very simple (although it does require a somewhat hard-to-find 4 pole, double-throw switch) but allows for instantly reversing the order of two effects so you can see what they sound like in two different orders.

ABOUT THE CIRCUIT

Switch S1 is the key to the circuit. If you trace through the schematic (Fig. 3-6), when S1a is in the 1 position, the input

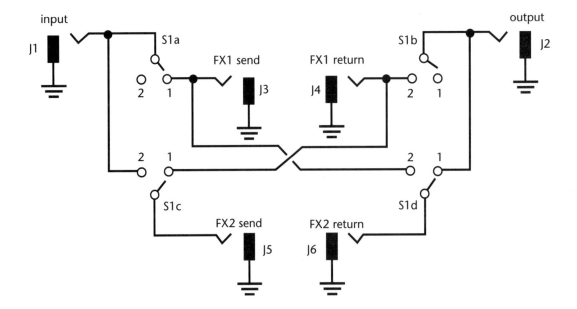

Fig. 3-6
Effects switcher
schematic.

connects to FX1 send J3 (this jack patches to the first effect's input). The first effect's output patches into the FX1 return, which connects through switch S1c to FX2 send J5; this patches to the second effect's input.

The second effect's output patches into J6 (FX2 return), which connects via S1d to the output jack. Thus with S1 in the "1" position, effect 1 precedes effect 2. If you trace through S1's wiring in the "2" position, effect 2 precedes effect 1.

This project fits well in a small aluminum project box. Just drill out the holes for the jacks and the switch, wire up the parts, and you're ready to go. If you have trouble locating a 4PDT toggle switch, use a rotary switch instead.

APPLYING THE EFFECTS ORDER SWITCHER

Here are some examples of what happens when you reverse the order of a pair of effects:

- **Compressor before distortion** increases sustain and gives a more consistent distortion timbre.

- **Distortion before compressor** tends to be a bit noisy but provides a somewhat "gentler" sound compared to compressor before distortion.

- **Pitch transposer before distortion.** The distortion doesn't quite know what to make of a polyphonic input signal, and will tend to produce a splattering, nasty type of distortion for any intervals except octaves and fifths.

- **Distortion before pitch transposer** gives a clean harmony sound since the pitch transposer synthesizes a second distortion signal.

- **Distortion before echo** gives a clear echo sound.

- **Echo before distortion** gives a muddy echo sound since the echoes all meld together when distorted.

- **Distortion before flanger or chorus.** Flangers and choruses give the most intense effect when they're fed a signal with lots of harmonics (overtones). Preceding them with distortion makes for a harmonically rich sound that enhances the flanging or chorusing effect.

- **Flanger or chorus before distortion.** Distortion pretty much masks the subtlety of the flanger or chorus effect.

PARTS LIST

S1	4PDT toggle or rotary switch
J1-J6	Mono, open circuit, ¼″ phone jacks
Misc.	Case, wire, solder, etc.

✳ *PROJECT* **5**
POWER/STATUS INDICATOR MONITOR

Is that effect really turned on? And if it is, is the effect active or bypassed—and do you really have to shorten a battery's life to find out? Not with this circuit.

Many battery-operated effects do not have power indicators, because LEDs can sometimes draw as much power as the effects box itself. The standard way to light an LED is to attach its anode to a resistor, which then connects to the positive supply voltage. The LED cathode connects to the negative supply voltage, or ground. The size of the resistor limits the amount of current going through the LED; for example, a 1k resistor with a 9V DC supply allows about 9 mA through the LED. Although an LED that only has 5 mA or so going through it is reasonably bright, pushing 8 to 10 mA through the LED is much brighter. Unfortunately, this amount of current is enough to eat up a battery pretty fast.

National Semiconductor's LM3909 LED flasher IC is one way to solve this problem. This IC flashes the LED at a fairly slow rate, but best of all, the average current consumption is only 0.5 mA. This low power operation doesn't make much of a dent in battery life, so there's no need to worry about the extra current drain. As a bonus, the blinking light draws your eye and reminds you that the power is on.

With some effects, this circuit can also be used as an effects status (in/out) indicator, as described later.

CONSTRUCTION

The circuit (Fig. 3-7) is about as simple as you can get. The 250μF capacitors need only be rated at 6V or so, which means that you can use fairly small electrolytic types. The 10k resistor is not really critical; increasing it decreases current consumption and brightness (and also requires a higher supply voltage range), while decreasing it to, for example, 4k7 increases current consumption and also increases brightness. The parts can either be soldered together and then put in something like a small plastic

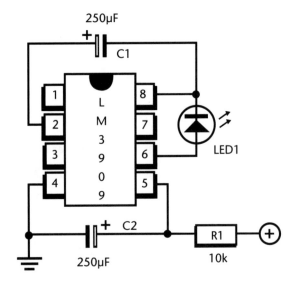

**Fig. 3-7
Power/status indicator schematic.**

case, or assembled on a piece of perf board. The LED should be mounted prominently on the effect.

The only important consideration when building the circuit Is to make sure that you orient the capacitors, IC, and LED correctly. Each capacitor will have a small (+) near one of the wires; this wire corresponds to the (+) side of the capacitor, and must hook up as shown in the schematic. It's also possible that the (-) lead will be marked instead of the (+); in this case, the unmarked lead is the (+) lead.

Regarding semiconductors, the IC will have a notch or dot along the top of the case. This must also be oriented as shown in the schematic for the circuit to work properly. The LED will have a flat side or dot near one lead; this is the cathode (which connects to pin 8 of the LM3909).

INSTALLATION

To indicate when power is supplied to an effect, clip the ground point of the monitor to ground, and the monitor's positive supply voltage point to the (+) power supply connection (for 9V battery connectors, this is the red lead). When the unit is turned on, the light will start flashing. If the light fails to flash, connect the monitor ground point to the (-) or black lead of the battery, and the monitor supply voltage point to the effect ground. If this still doesn't work, there's a wiring error or some other malfunction.

Using the monitor to indicate effect in/out status is some-what more complex, but here's the basic idea. Many effects use electronic signal switching; in this case, the footswitch simply switches a positive or negative voltage on or off with respect to ground, and feeds some of the effects box circuitry in the process.

To hook up the status indicator, first grab a voltmeter and attach the black probe to ground. Then, connect the red probe to one of the footswitch terminals (it will probably be an SPST footswitch). If switching the effect in gives a positive reading of more than +5V DC and switching the effect out gives a reading of around 0 Volts, you can use this circuit. Attach the monitor ground point to ground, and the monitor supply point to where you just had the voltmeter's red lead.

If the voltage doesn't change when you switch the effect in and out, try the other footswitch terminal and run the same procedure. If switching in the effect gives a negative reading of more than -5V DC, and switching the effect out gives a reading of 0V, you're still okay. In this instance, connect the monitor ground point to the footswitch terminal, and the monitor supply point to the effect ground. If performing the above steps doesn't produce results similar to what we're describing, resign yourself to not using the monitor as an effect in/out status indicator.

USING
THE MONITOR

When used as a power indicator, the flash rate and brightness give a good idea of battery strength. As the batteries age, the brightness will diminish and the rate will slow down. So, if you have several of these installed in something like a pedalboard and one is flashing at a much slower rate than the others, better be prepared to change the battery real soon. This feature is particularly handy with guitars using on-board electronics, because you can monitor the battery status and still add negligible current consumption. Incidentally, current consumption is less than 0.5 mA with supply voltages under 9V, while greater supply voltages draw somewhat more current (with a 15V supply voltage, the current drain increases to about 1.5 mA).

That's pretty much all there is to an inexpensive and simple status monitor LED. Whether to retrofit older effects or to indicate the status of a homemade device, this circuit does the job.

PARTS LIST

R1	10k resistor, any wattage rating
C1, C2	250µF electrolytic capacitors, 6V or more
D1	Red LED
IC1	LM3909 LED flasher (National Semiconductor)

✳ PROJECT 6
STEREO/MONO BREAKOUT BOX

Sometimes the simple projects are the most useful. If you use mixers with insert jacks, this little adapter box can make your life a lot easier.

In the studio, you'll sometimes want to patch your effects into a mixer channel's insert jacks if you want to process a guitar on mixdown, or if you're using high-end multieffects that can cope with the higher levels at the insert jacks (which results in less overall noise). The only problem is that a lot of mixers use stereo insert jacks to save space and money, and it's up to you to figure out how to interface your mono input and output connections to the stereo insert jack.

To complicate matters, insert jacks are not always wired in a standardized way; some use the tip connection for the signal send, and some for the signal return. But you can interface with any type of insert jack by building the Stereo/Mono Breakout Box (Fig. 3-8).

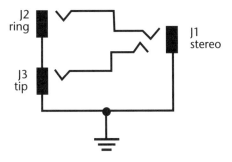

Fig. 3-8
Stereo/Mono Break-
out Box schematic.

CONSTRUCTION

Mount the circuit in a small aluminum box. You'll need two ¼" mono phone jacks and one ¼" stereo jack. Wire one mono jack hot lead to the stereo jack tip connection, the other mono jack hot lead to the stereo jack ring connection, then connect all the grounds together.

USING THE STEREO/MONO BREAKOUT BOX

Patch a stereo cord between the mixer's insert jack and J3, then patch mono jacks J2 and J3 to your signal processor in and out connections. If you don't get the tip and ring connections right the first time, reverse them and you should get signal.

PARTS LIST

J1	Stereo, open circuit, ¼" phone jack
J2, J3	Mono, open circuit, ¼" phone jacks
Misc.	Enclosure, wire, solder, etc.

4

Buffers & Preamps

✳ PROJECT 7
BUFFER BOARD

*Effects, amplifiers, and even cables may be robbing your guitar of
level, high end, and a "fat" sound. Here's a project that isolates your
guitar's pickups from the rest of your system, thus allowing them to
operate at maximum efficiency. You'd be amazed what this can do
for your sound.*

Project 28, Testing Impedance, explains why trying to feed
a low impedance output from a guitar with non-active pickups
can seriously degrade the overall sound quality. This Buffer Board
patches between your guitar and the first effect in the signal
chain; this not only prevents impedance matching problems that
can dull your sound, but is almost essential when creating a
parallel effects system (as described later in this project).

ABOUT THE CIRCUIT

Fig. 4-1 shows the schematic. IC1 can be a common 741 op
amp, or for improved performance, use an LF351, TL071 (for
extra-low noise), or TL081 op amp. The capacitors should be
rated at 10 or more volts, and the resistors should be 5% tolerance types.

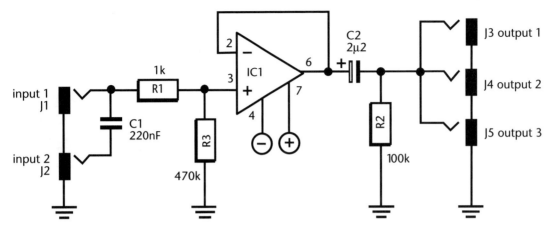

Fig. 4-1

Buffer Board

schematic.

Regarding the functions of the individual parts, R1 protects the op amp from static electricity, which can be a problem if you walk across a carpet on a dry day and then touch the end of a cord plugged into one of the inputs. R3 provides a high input impedance when using input 2, and R2 prevents capacitor C2 from building up a charge. This eliminates "popping" when you plug into the outputs.

Fig. 4-2 shows a suitable power supply using two 9V batteries (you can also use the AC Power Supply, Project #12). The power supply capacitor values (C3 and C4) are non-critical; anything from 5µF to 100µF will work. On-off switch S1 can be DPST or DPDT, depending on what's available.

Fig. 4-2

Battery power supply

for the Buffer Board.

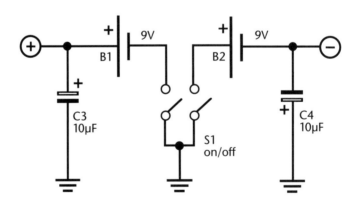

USING THE BUFFER BOARD

Although the Buffer Board can really clean up your signal, you don't get something for nothing. The op amp adds a little bit of noise (although this is pretty negligible compared to the noise contributed by later devices). Another caution is that a circuit

DO-IT-YOURSELF PROJECTS FOR GUITARISTS

with a high input impedance is more susceptible to hum and noise pickup; and if you're feeding the buffer with a shoddy cable that has a high internal capacitance, you can lose treble. Describing how cable capacitance affects frequency response is beyond the scope of this book, but suffice it to say that you should use the best quality shielded cable you can find between the guitar and Buffer Board.

The Buffer Board has two inputs. Plug into J1 for the lowest possible noise; however, if you encounter problems (popping, distortion, or hiss), plug into J2. The choice of inputs is not all that critical, so try both inputs until you decide which one works best.

Output jacks J3, J4, and J5 patch to subsequent inputs (effects, amplifier, mixer, etc.). The reason for using several paralleled output jacks is for use with parallel effects systems (see next section). Note that the multiple output jacks also provide direct outs for feeding devices such as tuners or tape recorder inputs.

One final consideration: if you get radio frequency interference, add a 10pF capacitor in parallel with resistor R3. This shunts frequencies above 30 kHz to ground.

ABOUT SERIES AND PARALLEL EFFECTS

There are two main ways of hooking effects together. Fig. 4-3 shows a typical *series* connection of effects, so called because the effects string together one after another in a serial fashion. The instrument plugs into the input of effect 1, effect 1's output plugs into effect 2's input, effect 2's output plugs into effect 3's input, and so on.

**Fig. 4-3
Four effects connected in series.**

Fig. 4-4 shows a *parallel* effects combination that splits the guitar into the inputs of effects 1 and 2. Mixing the outputs of the two effects together gives the combined (paralleled) sound of these effects. This connection is a little more complex than

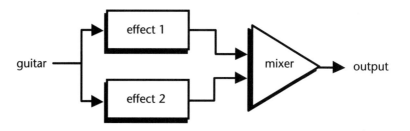

Fig. 4-4
Two effects con-
nected in parallel.

series connections, because we now need an additional mixer submodule.

Parallel effects combinations can provide a greater degree of subtlety than series combinations. As one example, putting bass through a serial effects combination consisting of chorus and envelope controlled filter will often give a thin sound because the filter removes the bass "bottom." Placing the envelope controlled filter in parallel with the chorused signal *adds* the filtered effect to the chorused bass sound (which doesn't remove the low end).

Parallel effects chains are also a good way to create a stereo image, since one leg of the chain can provide one channel and the other leg, the other channel. For example, suppose you feed your guitar into two 8-band graphic equalizer modules connected in parallel. If you set bands 1, 3, 5, and 7 to maximum and bands 2, 4, 6, and 8 to minimum in one channel, and do the reverse for the other channel (bands 1, 3, 5, and 7 to minimum with bands 2, 4, 6, and 8 to maximum), you'll create a big stereo spread.

However, a problem with parallel effects is that two effects load down a guitar more than one effect, which makes it even more necessary to have an electronic buffer. Inserting the Buffer Board into the effects chain not only minimizes the effects of loading, but provides separate feeds for the parallel effects (Fig. 4-5).

Fig. 4-5
Adding the Buffer
Board improves per-
formance in multiple
effects systems.

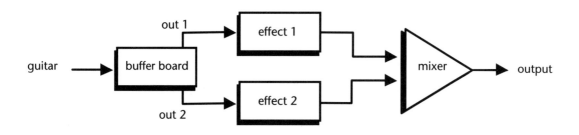

PARTS LIST

Resistors (1/4 watt, 5% or 10% tolerance)

R1	1k
R2	100k
R3	470k

Capacitors (10 working volts or greater)

C1	0.22µF (220nF) disc or mylar
C2	2.2µF (2µ2) electrolytic or tantalum
C3, C4	10µF electrolytic or tantalum

Other parts

IC1	See text
J1-J5	Mono, open circuit, ¼" phone jacks
S1	DPST or DPDT switch (see text)
Misc.	Batteries, battery connector, case, wire, solder, etc.

✳ *PROJECT* **8**
"CLARIFIER" ON-BOARD PREAMP/EQ

The Clarifier is a no-compromise preamp, small enough to mount in many guitars, that also includes active bass and treble equalization. Quiet and transparent-sounding, it boasts excellent specs and adds both clarity and punch to your sound.

The Clarifier squeezes a lot of performance out of a limited number of parts. With one IC, eight resistors, nine capacitors, three pots and some miscellaneous hardware, you can replace a guitar's standard passive tone control with a two control, active equalization circuit that provides over 12 dB of bass and treble boost and up to 6 dB of bass and treble cut. Some of the Clarifier's main features are:

- Buffers your pickups from external loading caused by cables and amp inputs, giving additional output and improved high frequency response.

- Adds a nominal 6 dB of gain to give your signal a bit more punch, as well as improve the signal-to-noise ratio in multiple effects systems.

- Prevents the volume control from interacting with the guitar pickups and cable—no more "dead spots" or tonal changes when you change volume.

- Runs on one or two batteries so you can choose between smallest size or greatest headroom, or run off +15 Volts for studio or synthesizer setups.

With a few modifications, the Clarifier can also serve as a simple equalizer for home recording, be built into amplifiers lacking tone controls, or turn into a "stomp box" for pedalboard setups. Perhaps best of all, this is a relatively simple circuit that is not expensive or critical to build.

SPECIFICATIONS

The signal-to-noise ratio (unweighted) is better than -85 dB, and better than -82 dB even with the treble control at maximum boost. Current drain depends on the op amp you choose, but is typically under 3 mA for low noise ICs and under 1 mA for low current ICs (although these generally have higher noise).

Concerning frequency response for the circuits given in Figs. 4-7 through 4-9 (all figures are referenced to the output signal with both controls flat), with the bass control at full boost there is +16 dB of gain at 50 Hz and +14 dB at 100 Hz. The boost becomes progressively less at higher frequencies until above about 3 kHz, response is essentially flat.

With the bass control at full cut, the cut starts taking effect around 3 kHz and is down -6 dB below about 200 Hz. With the treble control up full, there is +12 dB of gain at 10 kHz and +7 dB of gain at 4 kHz. The boost becomes progressively less at lower frequencies; below about 150 Hz, response is essentially flat.

With the treble control at full cut, the cut starts taking effect at about 150 Hz and response is down -6 dB above about 10 kHz. With the circuit in Fig. 4-10, boost figures are similar; however, the cutting action is much deeper (up to at least 12 dB for both the bass and treble controls).

So much for specs. Before getting into how to build the thing, here's some info for the wireheads among you on what makes this particular active EQ different from the norm.

STANDARD EQ VS. THE CLARIFIER

Most bass/treble, boost/cut circuits have a relatively low input impedance, which tends to load down guitar pickups. As a result, many onboard EQ circuits include two stages: one to buffer the guitar from the tone control, and the tone control itself. This circuit requires only one stage, which lowers noise, current consumption, and distortion compared to the standard design.

So what's the catch? With the single op amp circuits shown in Figs. 4-7 through 4-9, preserving a suitably high input impedance limits the bass/treble cut to a maximum of 6 dB. You still have full boost capabilities, though, and since more musicians seem interested in boosting than cutting, this is not much of a problem.

The other difference between this circuit and the standard type is that in our version, there's 6 dB of gain through the circuit with the bass and treble controls flat (standard tone controls, as well as the version of the Clarifier shown in Fig. 4-10, have unity gain with both controls flat). Actually, this is more of an advantage than a disadvantage since your instrument gets a subtle, but helpful, volume boost. If you find the extra level objectionable, no problem: just trim back the volume control.

That takes care of as much theory as we really need (or care!) to deal with. Now, let's move on to how to build it.

BUILDING THE CLARIFIER

Begin by mounting the required parts on a circuit board or piece of "perf" board (refer to the schematic in Fig. 4-6).

After completing the module, wire it into your axe. Probably the best approach is to wire the Clarifier to the outboard components, then mount all components inside your guitar. The main trick here is to make sure that the wires are long enough to allow

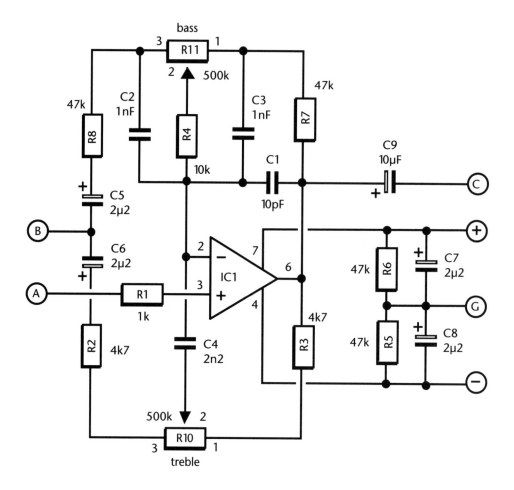

Fig. 4-6
Clarifier schematic.

the board pads to reach the outboard components, but not so long that they create a rat's next of wire inside your axe.

You'll need a special switching jack since using the battery configuration (whether you use one or two batteries) precludes using a standard stereo jack to turn the power on and off. Jacks are available (such as Mouser part #161-3503) that include independent SPST or SPDT switches; these either close or open, depending on the design, when you insert a plug. Unfortunately these parts are difficult to find, so you may have to use a potentiometer with an on-off switch on the back instead.

Attach the bass and treble controls, and you're ready to deal with pads A, B, C, G, (+), and (-). In the following figures, the bass and treble controls are not shown to make the diagram simpler.

Fig. 4-7 shows how to wire up the Clarifier as an on-board EQ unit for guitar or bass, with one 9V battery supplying power. Remove any guitar electronics between the pickup switch and output jack. Connect the lead which normally connects the

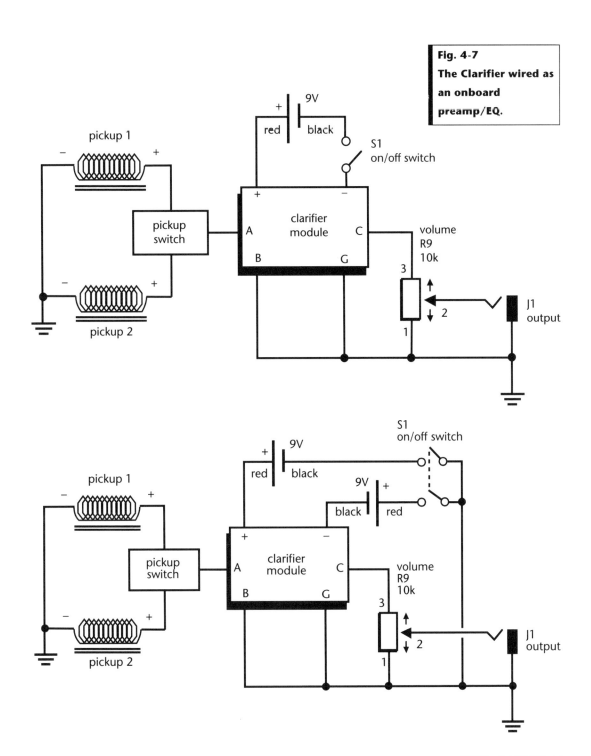

Fig. 4-7
The Clarifier wired as
an onboard
preamp/EQ.

pickup switch to the rest of the guitar electronics to pad A. With a Strat-like guitar, replace the three existing controls with the new bass, treble, and volume controls, and replace the regular output jack with the switching jack.

Fig. 4-8 shows the same basic idea, but using two batteries. Two batteries give greater headroom, which may be important if you have extra high output pickups or bash your strings

Fig. 4-8
The Clarifier wired up as an onboard device with two batteries.

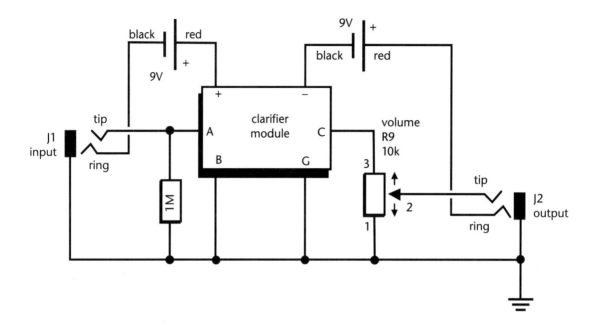

Fig. 4-9

Wiring the Clarifier inside an external box.

real hard. Now you need a DPST switch, which will probably require a potentiometer with an on/off switch or separate toggle power switch.

If you can't fit the circuit inside your guitar, then your only option is to mount it in an external box. This foregoes some of the benefits of on-board installation, but overall this is an acceptable compromise as long as you use a short cord between the guitar and Clarifier.

Fig. 4-9 shows how to wire up the Clarifier inside something like a small metal box. Don't ignore the 1 Meg resistor—this keeps the op amp happy when nothing's plugged into the input. Two stereo jacks, for the input and output, turn the batteries on when standard mono plugs are inserted in both jacks. This means that for maximum battery life, both plugs must be unplugged. An alternative is to use a DPST on/off switch, as in Fig. 4-8.

To use the circuit as part of a mixing console or similar piece of equipment, refer to Fig. 4-10. The Clarifier must now be driven by a low impedance output (*e.g.,* the output of a previous preamp, bus output, etc.). This particular wiring configuration provides full cut as well as full boost characteristics, and unlike the previous examples, there is unity gain through the system when the controls are flat.

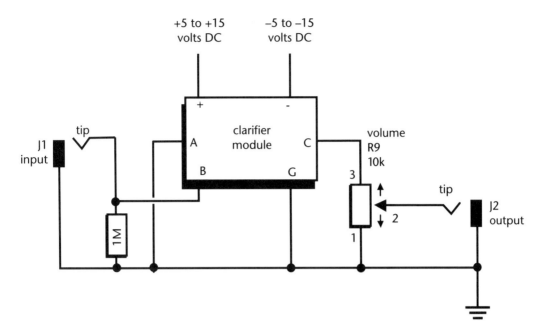

+5 to +15 volts DC   −5 to −15 volts DC

clarifier module

J1 input

tip

A
B
+
−
C
G

1M

volume
R9
10k

3
2
1

tip

J2
output

You can tap power from the mixing board to power the Clarifier, since the unit draws little current. Optionally, you could use two batteries.

Incidentally, if your guitar includes four controls you might wonder what to do with the leftover hole. With single battery versions, consider replacing the fourth control with a switch that can select between two batteries (as mentioned previously) in case one dies while you're on stage.

Speaking of modifications, here's one more tip. Because guitar and bass are relatively low frequency instruments, the Clarifier's treble range turnover point is also fairly low. For recording applications, you might want to change C4 to a lower value to raise the turnover point to a higher frequency.

All in all, this is a hot circuit that can definitely help clean up your sound. Check it out—the investment is minimal, but the sound is maximal.

**Fig. 4-10
Studio version; this requires a bipolar ±5 to ±15V DC power supply, such as the AC Power Supply (Project #12).**

PARTS LIST

Resistors	(5 or 10% tolerance, 1/4 watt)
R1	1k
R2, R3	4.7k (4k7)
R4	10k
R5 - R8	47k
R9	10k audio taper pot
R10, R11	500k linear taper pot

PARTS LIST *(continued)*

Capacitors (15 or more working volts)

C1	10pF ceramic disk
C2, C3	1000 pF (1nF) polystyrene
C4	2000 pF or 2200 pF (2nF or 2n2) polystyrene
C5 - C8	2.2 µF (2µ2) electrolytic
C9	10 µF electrolytic

Other parts

IC1	Texas Instruments TL071 op amp (low noise), or TL061 op amp (low current)
J1	Switching jack (see text)
Misc.	Solder, wire, knobs, circuit board, battery connector, etc.

✳ *PROJECT* **9**
BEAT THE DI BLUES WITH IGGY

When you need to interface with the pro world of balanced lines and XLR connectors, and don't need all the features of the Direct Injector (Project #21), reach for IGGY. But it can also do a lot more...

Here's the problem: typical guitars have high-impedance, unbalanced outputs that feed ¼" phone jacks, but most pro gear has low-impedance, balanced inputs that use XLR jacks. Trying to plug your axe into this kind of gear is like trying to fit a square peg in a round hole—or maybe "black hole" is more accurate, since a low impedance input will suck both clarity and level from your instrument.

This problem can also happen with ¼" unbalanced inputs that weren't designed with guitar in mind; the impedance is often low enough to decimate your decibels.

The usual solution is to either put up with rotten sound or spend big $$ on a pro-quality impedance/level converter device (although the Direct Injector project gives pro-quality for a lot less bucks). However, there's another option—for a little work and about $20 in parts, you can build IGGY (Interface Gizmo for Guitarists). It's more than just a studio device; here are some of its main applications:

- Patch your axe directly into console inputs to take advantage of the console's preamp, EQ, and easy patch bay interfacing.

- Drive pro-level signal processors that use XLR connectors.

- Drive balanced lines when you need long, interference-free cable runs.

- When patched between your guitar and a long unbalanced line, buffer pickups from high frequency losses caused by cable capacitance.

- Prevents any kind of low-impedance input, including poorly designed stomp boxes, from loading down your guitar pickups.

- If you're a real purist, you can also record right into the balanced inputs of tape recorders and DATs, thus bypassing all the mixer electronics completely (IGGY's signal-to-noise ratio is better than 90 dB). The difference in sound quality can be significant.

HOW IT WORKS

Fig. 4-11 shows the schematic; the main ground lines are drawn a little thicker. IC1 is an NE5532 dual low-noise op amp (this chip is used a lot in pro gear because of its excellent specs), however you can substitute a TL082 or TL072 (slightly lower noise than the 082) if the NE5532 is hard to find.

IC1a converts the guitar's output from high-impedance to low-impedance, while adding approximately 20 dB of gain. IC1b provides the additional output needed for balanced line operation. J2 sends the signal to unbalanced inputs, and J3 patches to balanced inputs. Since you can use both outputs simultaneously, IGGY is also an active splitter.

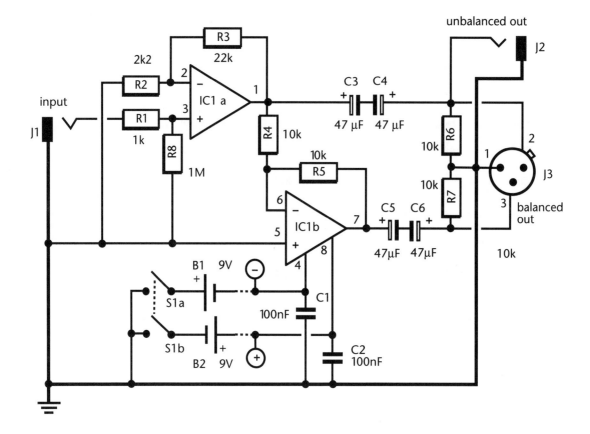

Fig. 4-11
IGGY's innards.

BUILDING IT

The simplest approach is to mount the parts on a perf board or printed circuit board, which then mounts inside a metal case that has a cable trailing out to an XLR plug or other plug. Install the ¼" jacks in the box itself. Use metal-film resistors for lowest noise, and a socket for IC1 to prevent heat damage while soldering.

Power IGGY with two 9V batteries as shown, or any bipolar power supply between +5 and +15V (*e.g.,* the AC Power Supply, Project #12). If you're not going to use batteries, remove them and S1 (which turns the battery power on and off); feed in the external supply at the points marked (+) and (-) on the schematic.

USING IT

Plug your guitar into J1 using as short a cable as possible, and patch J2/J3 into the console input, processor input, or long cable run. Play away; you might be surprised at just how clean and crisp a guitar can sound when it's not being loaded down.

MOD SQUAD

You can alter IGGY's gain by changing R3's value. The amount of gain equals (R3 + 2.2)/2.2, with R3 in kΩ. For example, R3 = 22k gives a gain of 11; 100k gives a gain of approximately 45.

J3 is wired with pin 2 "hot," in accordance with the IEC standard for XLR connectors. However, some maverick gear uses pin 3 as "hot." You can accommodate this gear by reversing the wires going to J3 pins 2 and 3, but this isn't really necessary unless you're using IGGY as a splitter.

And that's all there is to it. Aren't you glad you know how to solder?

PARTS LIST

Resistors   (5% tolerance, metal film preferred for fixed resistors)

R1	1k
R2	2.2k (2k2)
R3	22k
R4-R7	10k
R8	1M

Capacitors (35 or more working volts, mylar or polystyrene preferred except as noted)

C1, C2	0.1µF (100n)
C3-C6	47µF (tantalum or electrolytic)

Other parts

IC1-IC3	NE5532 or TL082 dual op amp
J1, J2	Mono, open circuit, ¼" phone jack
J3	XLR plug or chassis-mounting male XLR jack (see text)
S1a+b	DPST or DPDT switch
B1, B2	9-Volt battery (see text)
Misc.	IC socket, perf board, case, wire, power supply, etc.

SPECS

Frequency response: ±0.1 dB, 10 Hz - 100 kHz

S/N ratio: >90 dB

Input impedance: >500k Ohms

Output impedance: <600 Ohms

Headroom (+15V supply): >26V peak to peak

Gain: 20 dB

5

Cool Accessories

✳ *PROJECT* 10

THE FREQUENCY BOOSTER

Although there are many equalizers on the market, most are designed for general-purpose tone shaping. The Frequency Booster is a useful, quiet, easy-to-build equalizer designed especially for guitar that can boost your signal up to 12 dB at a selected frequency.

Different equalizers have different characteristic sounds, which is why some equalizers seem better-suited to certain instruments that others. This project provides a gentle bandpass response that sounds great with guitar. It's a really useful accessory when you want to punch through a track, boost a solo, or, when in the studio, help simulate the effect of going through a speaker cabinet.

WIRING THE CIRCUIT BOARD

First, choose the appropriate values for capacitors C1 and C2. These capacitors determine the filter's bandpass frequency (*i.e.,* where the response is boosted), and should be high quality mylar capacitors (5% or 10% tolerance) for best stability. The following values provide these different effects:

C1, C2 Value	Approx. Frequency	Net Effect
0.22µF (220nF)	90 Hz	bass boost ("rumble")
0.1µF (100nF)	200 Hz	low mid boost ("dark")
0.022µF (22nF)	1 kHz	mid boost ("honk")
0.01µF (10nF)	2 kHz	mid boost ("presence")
0.005µF (5nF)	4 kHz	upper mid boost ("sheen")

If you're enterprising, consider experimenting with different capacitor values, or using a switch to select one of several different capacitors.

Once you've decided on C1 and C2's values, mount all components except the controls, jacks, and switches on a piece of perf board, and wire them together using light gauge wire according to the schematic in Fig. 5-1. Use a socket for IC1.

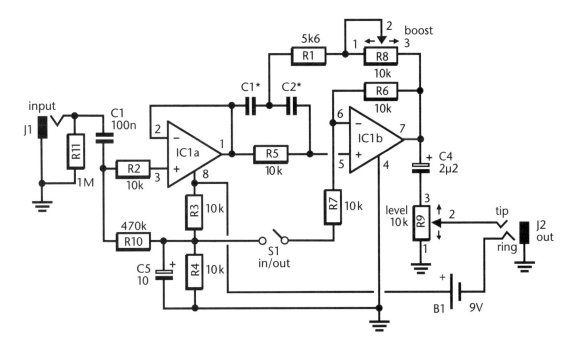

Carefully wire each part up as indicated; for example, pins 1 and 2 of IC1 connect to each other, as well as to one end of C1 and one end of R5. The other end of R5 connects to pin 5 of IC1 along with one end of C2, while the remaining terminals of C1 and C2 connect to each other and to R1. Remember to note C4 and C5's polarity and correctly identify IC1's pin numbers, or the Booster won't work correctly.

Fig. 5-1 Frequency Booster schematic.

J2 is a stereo phone jack, but this doesn't mean you're supposed to use a stereo cord—rather, we use this part so that plugging a cord into the Booster's output turns the battery on, and unplugging the cord turns the battery off. If you plug a standard mono cord into a stereo jack, you'll notice that one contact touches the plug's tip, while the other contact touches the plug's shaft. Trace each of these contacts to its matching lug. The lug associated with the contact that touches the plug's tip connects to R9's center terminal, while the other lug (ring) connects to the battery connector's black lead. The third lug, ground, which connects to the ground of the jack, goes to all points on the schematic marked with the ground symbol.

CONNECTING THE CIRCUIT BOARD TO THE OUTBOARD PARTS

Once you've wired up the circuit board, choose a suitable metal enclosure, drill holes for the pots, switch, and jacks, then connect wires from these outboard components to the circuit board. Don't forget to wire up the control terminals as described in the chapter on reading schematics. But if you wire up a control "backwards" so that the feel of the control is reversed, don't worry—just reverse the wires going to the two outside pot terminals.

APPLYING THE BOOSTER

Check your wiring carefully, then plug your axe into the input jack and patch the output jack to your amp. Opening S1 bypasses the effect. Closing S1 should give you a general volume boost, with R8 setting the amount of boost at the selected frequency. With R8 counterclockwise, you'll have about 3 dB of boost, and fully clockwise, a little over 12 dB—more than enough to make a fairly radical change in your instrument's sound.

PARTS LIST

Resistors (1/4 watt, 5% or 10% tolerance except as noted)

R1	5.6k (5k6)
R2—R7	10k
R8	10k linear taper pot
R9	10k audio or linear taper pot
R10	470k

Capacitors (10 working volts or greater)

C1, C2	Equal value mylar capacitors; see text
C3	0.1µF (100nF) disc ceramic
C4	2µ2 electrolytic
C5	10µF electrolytic

Other parts

IC1	NE5532, LF353, 5558, or equivalent dual op amp
J1	Mono, open circuit, ¼" phone jack
J2	Stereo, open circuit, ¼" phone jack
S1	SPST switch or footswitch
B1	9V transistor radio battery
Misc.	Battery connector, socket, circuit board, knobs, case, etc.

✳ *PROJECT* **11**
PHASE SWITCHER

Does your parallel effects system produce a thin sound instead of a nice, fat one? Maybe your effects are just going through a phase, and it's time for a switch. A phase switch, in fact.

The Buffer Board (Project #7) explains what parallel effects systems are, and why you might need a buffer to overcome the loading problems that can happen when a single output has to drive more than one effect. However, parallel effects systems are also subject to another problem: phase inconsistency.

Fig. 5-2 shows a simple parallel effects system with two effects, and a waveform feeding each effect. Effect 1's output is in phase with the input—in other words, when the input signal goes positive, the output signal goes positive. Effect 2's output

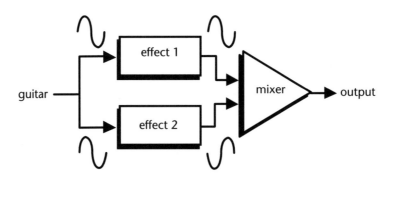

in phase + out of phase = no signal

in phase + in phase = stronger signal

is out of phase with the input; in this case, when the input signal goes positive, the output signal is inverted and goes negative.

Theoretically, the ear is not responsive to phase; it doesn't hear any difference whether a single effect's output is in or out of phase with the input. But the situation changes in a parallel effects system that mixes the output together. As the lower part of Fig. 5-2 shows, adding together an in-phase and out-of-phase signal gives zero signal. In practice, the output won't be exactly the same as the input, so the signals probably won't cancel completely. Instead, you'll just get a thinner sound. If you add two in-phase signals, you get a stronger signal.

Most engineers are aware that phase consistency is impor-tant, and design effects whose output is in phase with the input. Unfortunately, this was not the case with some vintage effects, and even today, some newer effects have phase

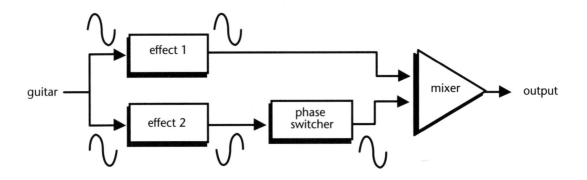

inconsistency. This isn't critical if the effect is used by itself, but problems crop up in parallel effects systems.

The answer is to insert a Phase Switcher to restore the proper phase (Fig. 5-3). By inverting the phase a second time, we end up with an in-phase signal, and all is well.

ABOUT THE CIRCUIT

The Phase Switcher (Fig. 5-4) can produce an output signal that's either in phase or out of phase with respect to the input, depending on S1's setting. With S1 in the (+) position, IC1 acts like a non-inverting, unity-gain buffer. In the (-) position, IC1 becomes an inverting amp with a gain of 1. Note that there is no output level change when you switch phase.

Fig. 5-4
Phase Switcher schematic.

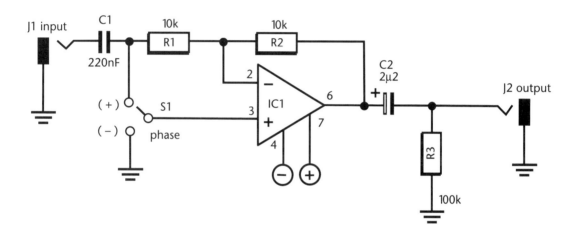

IC1 can be a common 741 op amp, or for improved performance, a TL071 or LF351. Power can be provided by two batteries (the circuit draws very little current), or the AC Power Supply project.

USING THE PHASE SWITCHER

In a parallel effects system, the Phase Switcher patches between the effect to be phase-changed and the mixer (Fig. 5-3). With S1 in the (+) position, the output is in phase with the input. With S1 in the (-) position, the output is out of phase with the input. Thus, if you have an effect with an out-of-phase output, and reverse the phase a second time with the Phase Switcher, the Phase Switcher output will be in phase with the effect input (got that?). Flick S1 back and forth, choosing whichever position gives the fullest sound. (However, note that switching an effect out of phase with respect to other effects can also produce some useful timbres—consider what out-of-phase switching does for pickups.)

The Phase Switcher can also be useful in the studio when using several mics to pick up an instrument. Sometimes a mic cable will be wired out of phase, or a microphone will be placed in a position where it produces an out-of-phase signal with respect to another microphone. Patch the Phase Switcher into one of the mic lines, and change the phase to see if you get a stronger sound.

PARTS LIST

Resistors (1/4 watt, 5% or 10% tolerance)

R1, R2	10k
R3	100k

Capacitors (10V or greater)

C1	0.22µF (220nF) disc
C2	2.2µF (2µ2) electrolytic

Other parts

IC1	TL071 (see text)
S1	SPDT (single pole, double throw) switch
J1, J2	Mono, open circuit, ¼" phone jacks

✳ PROJECT 12
AC POWER SUPPLY/BATTERY ELIMINATOR

If there's one thing most projects have in common, it's a lust for power. This supply not only does the job, but is short-circuit and thermally protected so it's almost impossible to damage.

This power supply is called bipolar because it produces both positive and negative voltages with respect to ground; it can deliver ±9V at up to 1/4 amp per side. That's enough to power every single project in this book simultaneously except for the Practice Amp, which requires its own dedicated supply. The AC

Power Supply will also work with many other effects that require 9V batteries, as described toward the end of this section.

HOW IT WORKS

Designing power supplies used to be an annoyance, until the advent of the IC voltage regulator (Fig. 5-5). These regulators take filtered (but unregulated) DC at their inputs, and magically deliver tightly regulated (stable) and virtually hum-free DC at their outputs. They are available in various fixed voltages (generally 5, 6, 8, 12, 15, 18, and 24 volts—both positive and negative), and adjustable versions. However, there are no 9-volt regulators, so we'll have to add a few extra parts to get our supply happening.

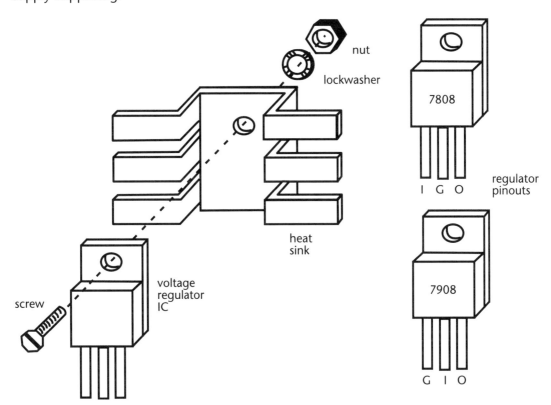

nut

lockwasher

7808

heat sink

regulator pinouts

I G O

voltage regulator IC

screw

7908

G I O

Referring to Fig. 5-6, we start off with a 20 to 24 volt center-tapped transformer, T1. Feeding the transformer secondary through a full-wave rectifier (diodes D1-D4) produces a DC voltage. The two filter capacitors (C1 and C2) smooth out the DC to get rid of ripple and hum; they also improve the supply's stability. The voltage at each capacitor must be at least 3V higher than the desired output voltage to properly feed the regulators.

Fig. 5-5
IC voltage regulator pinouts and heat sink mounting technique.

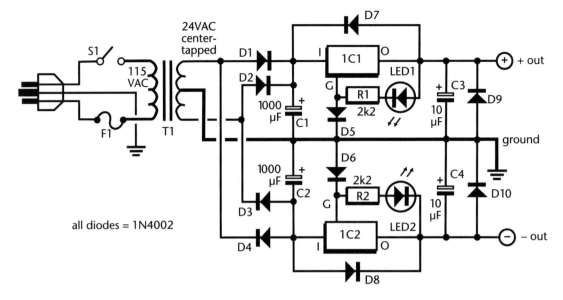

Fig. 5-6
Bipolar power supply schematic.

Since this voltage will depend on the current load, make sure your capacitors are suitably rated (25 working volts should be enough).

In the positive regulator section built around IC1, the positive unregulated voltage goes to the 7808's input. Although this is a +8V regulator, adding diode D5 between the ground pin and ground raises the voltage an additional 0.7V. The LED1/R1 combination insures adequate current flow through the diode to maintain an accurate reference, and the LED also indicates that the supply is working (when the LED lights, the supply is on).

Diode D7 protects IC1 if the output voltage should exceed the input, which can happen if the positive filter capacitor is accidentally discharged during operation. Diode D9 insures that only positive voltages appear at the output; any negative voltage shunts through the diode to ground.

The negative regulator section built around IC2 is very similar to the positive regulator, but uses an equivalent negative regulator IC, the 7908. Again we must change the operating voltage (to around -9V), and D6/LED2/R2 take care of this. Diodes D8 and D10 again perform protective functions, but are oriented differently because we are dealing with a negative regulator.

CONSTRUCTION TIPS

Unless the current demand is light (*i.e.,* you're powering only a few projects), the regulators must attach to heat sinks that dissipate excess heat. The general idea is to make sure the regulator's case makes thermal contact with a large chunk of metal; Fig. 5-1 shows how to attach a regulator to one popular heat sink design (heat sinks come in a variety of shapes and sizes). You may use a piece of scrap aluminum or the like, but make sure that the heat sinks do not touch ground or other components. In particular, keep them away from capacitors, which age faster when exposed to excessive heat. No extreme precautions are required—just don't stick the capacitors right up next to the sinks.

One great feature of IC voltage regulators is that they include both thermal protection and current limiting. If a regulator gets too hot, the IC shuts itself off without damage until it cools down enough to take the load again. If the power supply shuts down a lot or the regulator gets very hot, increase the size of the heat sink or reduce the current demand.

The way you ground the various connections is important. Use heavy gauge wire (*e.g.*, #20 or #22) for the common ground connection indicated with the thicker line, as well as the supply line connections. Connect the ground points for C1-C4, D5, D6, D9, and D10, as well as the output ground connection (indicated with the larger ground symbol) to the transformer's center tap through as short a wire as possible for the best results.

Now the most important part: *BE CAREFUL WHEN WORKING WITH AC VOLTAGES SINCE THEY CAN BE LETHAL!* Securely attach the AC line cord leads and the leads from the transformer primary to the fuse holder and S1. Also make sure that all AC connections are well away from the chassis and insulated (heat shrink tubing is best, since electrical tape may unravel over time); it's possible that someone could accidentally step on the chassis and cause a short circuit by shorting the case to the wiring. Although the fuse gives a certain amount of protection, it's important to always build anything that uses AC with an eye toward safety. *If you have any doubts whatsoever about your ability to complete this project, or are unfamiliar with proper AC power construction techniques, do not attempt to build this power supply.*

USING THE POWER SUPPLY

The various projects indicate (+), (-) and ground connections (some projects require only a + connection and ground). Hook the power supply (+) to the project's (+) connection, the power supply (-) to the project's (-) connection (if required), and the power supply ground to the project's ground connection through a relatively short wire, and you're ready to go.

Tired of dishing out money for batteries? I hope the above information helps.

PARTS LIST

Resistors (1/4 watt, 5% or 10% tolerance)
R1, R2   2.2k (2k2)

Capacitors
C1, C2   1000µF/25V electrolytic
C3, C4   10µF/10V electrolytic or tantalum

Semiconductors
D1-D10   1N4002 or equivalent power diode
IC1   7808 +8V regulator IC
IC2   7908 -8V regulator IC
LED1   Red LED
LED2   Green LED

Other parts
T1   115 VAC primary, 24 VAC center-tapped secondary
           @ 1A transformer
S1   SPST on-off switch rated at 125V minimum
F1   1/4 or 1/2A fast-blow fuse
Misc.   AC line cord, chassis, solder, wire, fuse holder,
           screws, etc.

✳ PROJECT **13**
AC-POWERED PRACTICE AMP

If you want to amplify your guitar backstage for tuning, practice in a hotel room, or just make peace with neighbors who don't appreciate your Marshall stack, this is the project for you.

Battery-powered practice amps can produce only so much power; trying to shove out lots of watts means having to shove in lots of batteries—and with today's battery costs, the expense becomes prohibitive. For applications where you need a bit more oomph, this AC-powered design does the job. It doesn't exactly deliver ear-shattering volume, but it does give a good clean sound at comfortable listening levels.

ABOUT THE CIRCUIT

This circuit is based around National Semiconductor's LM383 power amp IC, which can put out up to 8 watts. The actual amount of power depends upon what kind of speaker and power supply you use (or as they always say, "your mileage may vary..."). All other parts for the circuit are common, and should be available from Radio Shack and most mail-order electronics outfits.

CONSTRUCTION

The amp (Fig. 5-7) can be built in just about any type of suitable enclosure; you can even build the thing inside the speaker baffle that contains Spkr1. If you expect to use the practice amp

Fig. 5-7
AC Practice Amp schematic.

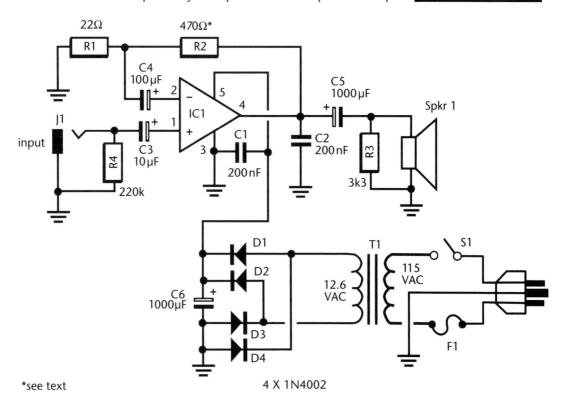

*see text   4 X 1N4002

with a number of different speakers, then build the amp inside a separate box and include a phone jack or similar connector to allow plugging in to the speaker of your choice.

There are a few cautions concerning this design. Since this is a relatively high power, high gain circuit, you have to be pretty careful about grounding and how you route the input and output leads. For best results, observe the following precautions:

- Build the amp inside a metal (aluminum preferred) case.

- Separate the input and output leads to avoid oscillation.

- Use a single point grounding system, where all grounds connect to one place. That one place should be the (-) end of capacitor C6, which also connects to chassis ground.

- Attach the LM383 to a heat sink. Since the LM383 case is at ground potential, you can simply attach it to the metal chassis and let the chassis conduct heat away from the IC. If you do not attach the LM383 to the chassis, then you should add a separate heat sink. By the way, the LM383 is short circuit and thermal overload protected, so if it ends up running too hot, it won't blow up but instead will shut down until it has a chance to cool off.

- Mount C1 close to the IC pins. This bypasses the power supply, which discourages oscillation and similar problems.

- Use a fuse in the AC supply leads as shown. This should be a 1/4A to 1/2A, fast-blow type.

- And now, for the standard don't-kill-yourself disclaimer: *BE CAREFUL WHEN WORKING WITH AC VOLTAGES SINCE THEY CAN BE LETHAL!* Securely attach the AC line cord leads and the leads from the transformer primary to the fuse holder and S1. Also make sure that all AC connections are well away from the chassis and insulated (heat shrink tubing is best, since electrical tape may unravel over time); it's possible that someone could accidentally step on the amp chassis and cause a short circuit by shorting the case to the wiring. Although the fuse gives a certain amount of protection, it's important to always build anything that uses AC with an eye toward safety. *If you have any doubts whatsoever about your ability to complete this project, or are unfamiliar with proper AC power construction techniques, do not attempt to build this amp.*

SPEAKER AND POWER SUPPLY

You have a couple of choices for Spkr1. The higher its impedance, the less power you'll get out of the circuit. A 4Ω speaker (or two paralleled 8Ω speakers) will work just fine; an 8Ω speaker is okay, but won't give you as much output. You can even parallel two 4Ω speakers for a total load of 2Ω. This gives the highest potential wattage.

While AC power is preferable for an amp like this, you can also run it from something like a 12-volt car battery or other heavy-duty DC power source (two 6-volt lantern batteries, for example). In this case, omit D2-D4; connect the battery's positive terminal to D1's cathode and the negative terminal to ground.

USING THE PRACTICE AMP

The procedure is pretty straightforward: plug in and if the thing doesn't work, check for errors. If you get distortion, though, you may need to change R2. It's shown as 470Ω, which gives a fair amount of gain and therefore lets you feed the amp directly with low level output instruments such as guitar. If you have an axe with on-board electronics or something else that generates a lot of output, then change R2 to around 270 or 220Ω.

Now all that remains is to…start practicing!

PARTS LIST

Resistors	(1/4 watt, 5% or 10% tolerance)
R1	22Ω
R2	220Ω to 470Ω (see text)
R3	3.3k (3k3)
R4	220k
Capacitors	(20 or more working volts)
C1, C2	0.22µF (220nF) ceramic or mylar
C3	10µF electrolytic or tantalum

PARTS LIST (continued)

C4	100µF electrolytic
C5, C6	1000µF electrolytic

Semiconductors

D1-D4	1N4002 or equivalent power diode
IC1	LM383 (National Semiconductor) power amp IC

Other parts

T1	115 VAC primary, 12.6 VAC secondary @ 1A transformer
S1	SPST on-off switch rated at 125V minimum
F1	1/4 or 1/2A fast-blow fuse
J1	Mono, open circuit, ¼" phone jack
SPKR1	2Ω to 8Ω speaker (see text)
Misc.	AC line cord, chassis, solder, wire, fuse holder, screws, etc.

✳ *PROJECT* **14**
THE SIGNAL SWITCHER

What do you do when you have several instruments but only one input to which you can feed them? Or you want to switch one guitar between several amps? Once again, do-it-yourself electronics comes to the rescue.

You know the problems that can occur when you use more than one guitar during a set. Not only can you get a horrible buzz when changing from one instrument to another, but there's also a certain lack of professionalism in spending a lot of time switching back and forth between guitars (or whatever instruments you might also play on stage).

The inspiration for this project came from a player who wanted to know about the feasibility of running three instruments through one wireless setup to cut down on cord entanglements. His idea was to put a signal switcher after the wireless receiver, and then route the signal to one of two direct boxes or a guitar amp. This seems like a rather atypical application; in most cases, I think you would probably want to switch the instruments going into the transmitter. In any event, this signal switcher is bi-directional—you can either switch three instruments down into one line, or switch one line into three different locations. For the latter application, just treat output jack J4 as the input, and input jacks J1-J3 as the three outputs.

HOW IT WORKS

Fig. 5-8 shows the Switcher's schematic. S1a switches output jack J4 to any of three input jacks (J1, J2, and J3), into which you plug your various instruments. S1b activates corresponding LEDs (one red, one green, and one yellow) to indicate which input is selected. For switching between more instruments, replace S1 with a switch having more throws (such as a double pole, six throw switch if you wanted to switch between six different instruments).

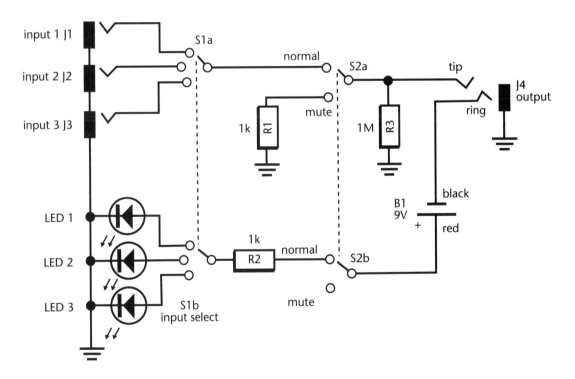

J4 is a stereo jack, although it's designed to be used with a mono cord. When you plug a mono plug into J4, the ring terminal connects to ground, thus connecting the negative end of B1 to ground and enabling the LED circuitry. Unplugging from J4 disconnects the battery; always unplug the output cord for longest battery life.

Fig. 5-8
Signal switcher
schematic.

Mute switch S2 is a DPDT toggle switch that, when in the mute position, insures that everything is nice and quiet when you switch between the various axes. S2a connects the output line to ground to provide the muting effect, while S2b turns off whichever LED is selected to show that you're in the mute mode.

HOW TO BUILD IT

This project is a good candidate for a small aluminum (not plastic!) minibox. Drill the holes, mount the parts, and wire 'em up—this is not a difficult project. For neatest results, mount the LEDs in little holders or grommets, and make sure they're polarized correctly (there will be a little flat spot or dot of paint near the cathode lead, which connects to ground).

HOW TO USE IT

Plug your instruments into J1-J3, and plug J4 into the cable leading to your amp, PA board, tape recorder, wireless transmitter, etc. Test each instrument to make sure that it comes through when selected, and that the LEDs light to indicate which instrument is selected.

Now play your selected instrument and flip S2 to the mute position; there should be no heavy-duty clicks or pops, and the sound should go away. Incidentally, operation will probably be quiet enough if you just switch with S1 so that you won't have to use S2, but there may be instances where the mute switch comes in handy.

As mentioned earlier, you can also use this box bi-directionally. For example, suppose you wanted to switch one guitar to three different amps. You'd plug your axe into J4, and connect J1-J3 to your amps. Also, if you want to also feed something like a direct box, no problem—just add another jack in parallel with J1, J2, J3, or J4 (whichever is appropriate) and tap off this jack with the direct box.

MODIFICATIONS

LEDs tend to draw a fair amount of current, so for the longest battery life, increase R2 (*e.g.,* to 1.5k) to push less current through the selected LED. Conversely, if you need real bright LEDs and don't mind replacing batteries more often, lower R2 to 680Ω or so (better yet, use a 9V battery eliminator or Project #12, AC Power Supply). To dispense with batteries altogether, simply eliminate the LEDs, R2, and B1, and ignore S1b and S2b.

So there it is—a simple signal switcher that will keep things quieter and less cluttered on stage. Now there's a switch!

PARTS LIST

Resistors   (1/4 watt, 5% or 10% tolerance)

R1, R2   1k

R3   1 Meg

Other parts

B1   9V transistor radio battery

J1-J3   Mono, open circuit, ¼" phone jacks

J4   Stereo, open circuit, ¼" phone jack

S1   2P3T rotary switch (see text)

S2   DPDT toggle switch

LED1-LED3   Standard LEDs—green, yellow, red

Misc.   Enclosure, knob, solder, wire, 9V battery connector, hardware, etc.

✳ *PROJECT* **15**
VOLUME PEDAL DE-SCRATCHER

Breakfast cereals are supposed to snap, crackle, and pop—not volume pedals. If you want the smoothest and quietest volume pedal action around, this circuit is the ticket.

Most standard volume pedals wire a volume control between an input and output jack (Fig. 5-9); unfortunately, there are two serious problems with this design. Eventually, the pot can become worn (thus adding crackles to your sound), and in some cases the tone of your guitar can change as you change volume. The Volume Pedal De-Scratcher (VPD for short) solves both problems.

Simply take any old pedal that's wired as shown in Fig. 5-9, modify it a bit, then add the VPD circuitry...and you'll end up

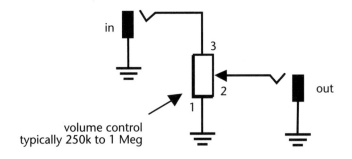

Fig. 5-9
Typical passive (non-optoisolator) volume pedal wiring.

in

3

2

1

out

volume control
typically 250k to 1 Meg

with one of the best-behaved pedals around. Not only will you not have to worry about scratchy pots or unexpected tonal changes, but the "action" of the pedal will be very even as you vary the pedal from full off to full on. And despite its simplicity and low cost, the VPD is no slouch when it comes to specs (see "Specifications").

HOW IT WORKS

You don't need to read this section to build the VPD, but tracing through the circuit can help you understand how it works. Referring to Fig. 5-10, IC1 is the heart of the VPD. This IC is like other op amps except that pin 5 is a control terminal; sending more current into this terminal increases the op amp's gain. With minimum current, IC1 is at minimum gain, and with maximum current, IC1 is at maximum gain. This phenomenon is called *transconductance,* and the CA3080 is an example of an operational transconductance amplifier (OTA for short). While this particular OTA is a fairly old part, you can't beat it for price—and the performance is pretty good.

The CA3080 has a high output impedance, and likes to "see" about a 100k load. IC2 provides this load via R6, and also buffers the output to provide a low impedance output suitable for driving mixers, amplifiers, tape recorders, etc.

To power the circuit from a single 9V battery, R1 and R2 form a voltage divider with one-half of the supply voltage appearing at their junction. This supplies an artificial "ground" that fools the op amps into thinking that they are being powered by a ±4.5V bipolar supply rather than the +9V unipolar supply provided by a battery. D2 acts as a polarity reversal protector in case battery B1 is inserted incorrectly.

DO-IT-YOURSELF PROJECTS FOR GUITARISTS

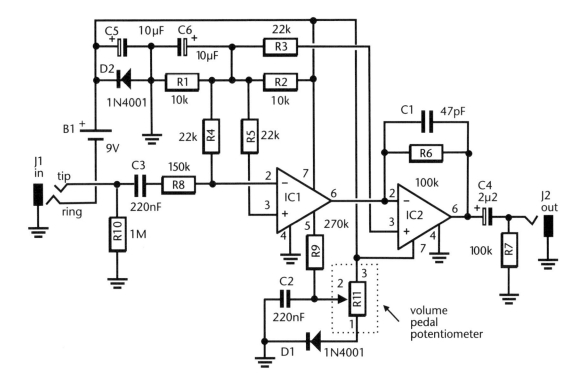

Fig. 5-10
VDP schematic.

The volume pedal pot varies the amount of current going into pin 5 of the CA3080. Diode D1 is necessary to counteract a "dead spot" in the control current response of the CA3080 as it approaches minimum gain, while C2 helps slow down the response of the pedal a bit so that any transients (snaps or pops) are absorbed by this capacitor rather than going into pin 5 and causing audible problems.

BUILDING THE VPD

Pay special attention to the wiring of stereo jack J1, and do not use a stereo cord with this jack. J1 is wired so that it acts as both the input jack to the circuit and an on-off switch—plug into the input jack and the VPD turns on, unplug and the VPD turns off. The jack's tip connection should mate with the tip of the plug plugged into J1, while the ring lug should contact the plug's ground.

Also check the polarity of the electrolytic capacitors and diodes (these must be oriented properly or the VPD will not work), and note that pins 1 and 8 on IC1 and pins 1, 5, and 8 on IC2 should not connect to anything. Make sure both ICs are oriented properly. IC2 can be any 741-type pinout op amp such as the LF351, LF356, TLO71, etc. Of these ICs the 741 will give the noisiest performance, but it will do in a pinch. Use sockets for both IC1 and IC2.

REWIRING THE VOLUME PEDAL

Once you've built the VPD circuit, you're almost ready to go. Referring to Fig. 5-1, note which pedal pot wires correspond to terminals 1, 2, and 3, then reconnect these wires to the VPD as indicated on the schematic. Replace the pedal input jack with a stereo jack, and wire the input and output jacks to the VPD as indicated. Make sure that you also have a ground connection going from the VPD to the volume pedal's outside metal shell.

CHECKING OUT THE VPD

There's not much to this: plug your guitar into the input, plug the output to an amp, and vary the pedal. You should hear a quiet, smooth transition as you change volume levels with the pedal; if you encounter problems, shut down power immediately and recheck your wiring.

There are some modifications you can do to optimize performance. If the unit distorts on peaks of your playing, decrease R4's value until the distortion goes away. Conversely, if the unit seems noisy, this usually means there's not enough gain—increase R4 as much as possible short of distortion. If you anticipate using instruments with widely varying output levels, consider replacing R4 with a 100k trimpot (or standard potentiometer) in series with a 1k resistor.

To make the pedal action even more smooth, increase C2's value. However, too large a value creates a time lag when you change volume rapidly.

Well, that's it for the VPD. It's useful, it's inexpensive, and it works. May your pedal never crackle and spit at you again.

SPECIFICATIONS

Current drain with 9V supply: Typically 1 mA (varies depending on the op amp selected for IC2)

Operating voltage range: +6 to +10V DC

Frequency response: +1 dB, 10 Hz to 20 kHz

Signal-to-noise ratio at maximum gain: 70 dB

Input/output phase relationship: In-phase

Input impedance: Greater than 120k

Output impedance: Less than 1k

Pedal full on/full off dynamic range @ 1 kHz: 75 dB

PARTS LIST

Resistors   (5%, 1/4 watt except as indicated)

R1, R2	10k
R3-R5	22k
R6, R7	100k
R8	150k
R9	270k
R10	1M
R11	Volume pedal pot

Capacitors (10 or more working volts)

C1	47pF disc ceramic
C2, C3	0.22µF (220nF), mylar preferred
C4	2.2µF (2µ2) electrolytic
C5, C6	10µF electrolytic

Semiconductors

D1, D2	1N4001 silicon diode
IC1	CA3080 op amp
IC2	TL071 or equivalent op amp (see text)

Other parts

J1	Stereo, open circuit, ¼" phone jack
J2	Mono, open circuit, ¼" phone jack
B1	9V battery
Misc.	Two 8 pin sockets, battery connector, circuit board, wire, parts, solder, etc.

6

Guitar Rewirings

✱ PROJECT 16
CHEAP 'N' CHEERFUL TONE MODS

If you're looking for some inexpensive and simple ways to improve your overall sound, you can't get much easier than the following modifications. Best of all, they may help you achieve a sound that's truly your own.

You don't always need a lot of fancy electronic gadgets to make a big difference in the sound of a guitar; many times some simple pickup adjustments or rewirings are all that's necessary. Just remember that although these modifications are pretty easy, be extremely careful when working on a guitar—you don't want any solder blobs to mess with the finish.

PICKUP POSITIONING

Most people know that the distance between a pickup and the strings influences overall output; moving the pickup closer to the string produces more output. Height adjustment usually involves turning two screws located on the side of the pickup.

However, it's just as important to make sure that the treble and bass strings are balanced, which may require raising one side of the pickup higher than the other. Because the ear is not real good at discriminating between differences in level, when adjusting pickups I feed the guitar into a device with an LED VU meter (such as Project #29, the LED Level Meter) to get some visual feedback.

What's less commonly known is that with pickups containing adjustable-screw pole pieces, you can make a pickup's character brighter or bassier depending on how the pole pieces are adjusted (thanks to pickup pioneer Dan Armstrong for this tip). If you're willing to trade off overall level for more treble, screw the pole pieces somewhat out of the pickup body and lower the pickup to compensate for the extra height. If you're willing to trade off "definition" for a bassier, louder sound, screw the pole pieces into the pickup body and bring it up close to the strings. After making these "ballpark" adjustments, trim each pole piece to even out level differences between strings.

Speaking of strings, I prefer the sound of heavier gauge strings and you might too. Using a 0.010 set instead of a 0.009 set doesn't require that much more finger strength, yet gives a bit more output. (I also break strings a lot less often with heavier gauge strings.)

TONE CONTROL VARIATIONS

A few modifications can make passive tone controls far more effective. Most passive guitar circuits use a tone control design similar to the one shown in Figs. 1A and 1B. The tone control may connect directly across a pickup if each pickup has its own tone control (Fig. 6-1A), or just before the volume control if there's a single tone control (Fig. 6-1B). In either case, the theory of operation is the same. The capacitor (typically 0.02μF) "drains" high frequencies to ground, so with R1 at minimum

Fig. 6-1

Standard tone control circuits.

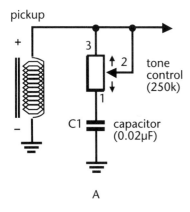

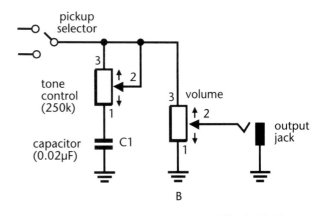

A   B

Fig. 6-2

How to get three distinctly different sounds with a single tone control.

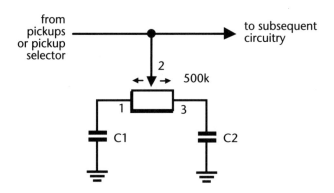

resistance, the capacitor connects directly across the audio line and shunts highs to ground. With R1 at maximum resistance, the capacitor is, for all practical purposes, taken out of the circuit and therefore leaves the highs alone.

Increasing the capacitor value to 0.03µF or 0.05µF shunts more highs to ground when R1 is at minimum resistance, creating a bassier tone. This is great for getting a real smooth fuzz sound—less highs leads to a silkier distortion effect. If, on the other hand, your tone control has too drastic an action, reduce the capacitor's value.

To "have your cake and eat it too," try the circuit in Fig. 6-2. Setting R1 to one extreme of its rotation puts one of the capacitors across the audio line, setting R1 to the opposite extreme puts the other capacitor across the audio line, and setting R1 in the middle takes the capacitors out of the circuit. This gives three distinctly different sounds without having to drill any new holes in your axe (although if R1 is a 250k pot, you'll probably want to replace it with a 500k pot to insure that the capacitors are out of the circuit when the pot wiper is at its midpoint). Try 0.01µF for one capacitor and 0.02µF to 0.05µF for the other.

BRIGHTER RHYTHM GUITAR SOUNDS

Turning down your guitar's volume often turns down the guitar's "presence" as well. There's an easy solution: referring to Fig. 6-3, wire a 0.001µF (1nF) capacitor between the volume control's "hot" and "wiper" terminals. As you turn down the volume, the capacitor lets some of the highs through directly to the output, bypassing the volume control. The more you turn down the vol-

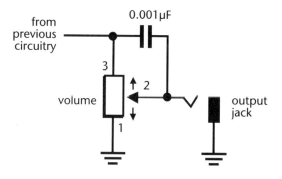

Fig. 6-3
Add a capacitor across the volume control to increase highs as you turn down the volume.

ume, the greater the percentage of highs in the overall sound. This trick has been used for years with some very popular guitars—give it a try. If the effect isn't obvious enough, use a 0.002µF (2nF) capacitor.

LOW CUT FILTER

Most tone controls remove highs, but if you're looking for a thinner, brighter sound, here's a tone control that removes lows (Fig. 6-4). With the low cut control at maximum resistance, C1 lets through highs but attenuates low frequencies. Setting the control to minimum resistance shorts out the cap and restores normal operation.

C1 can range from 470pF to 0.002µF, depending on the type of amp you're feeding, the value of the volume control, etc. As always, experiment until you find the sound that's right for you.

Fig. 6-4
A low cut tone control, shown along with an optional high cut (standard) tone control.

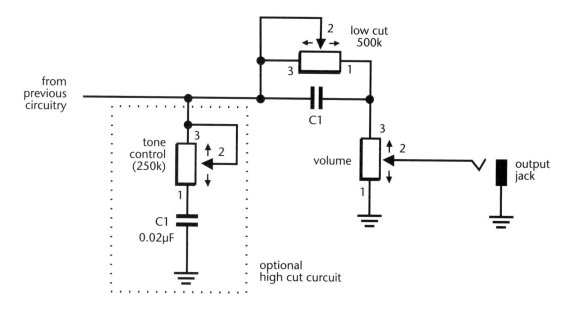

COIL TAP "SWITCH"

Some players use single coil pickups that include a center tap. This can give two sounds from one pickup, since connecting the tap to ground cuts the volume a bit and gives more highs, while leaving the tap open gives the standard single coil pickup sound.

Players who favor humbuckers can tap a wire off the connection between the two coils, and connect that wire to a switch to ground. Closing this switch disables one of the humbucker coils, thus creating a single coil pickup sound.

Unfortunately, both of these techniques require an additional switch. However, some Peavey guitars get around the need for an extra switch with an elegant, yet simple, guitar wiring scheme patented by inventor "Red" Rhodes in 1979. (While this patent was assigned to Peavey Electronics, note that individual experimenters may use patented circuits for their own private, non-commercial use without fear of infringement.)

Fig. 6-5
Setting up a control to serve double duty: control tone, and switch the coil tap in and out.

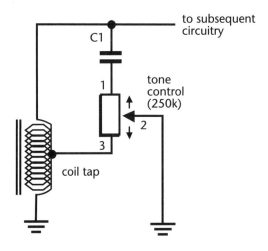

Fig. 6-5 shows what's going on. With the tone control fully counterclockwise (terminal 2 connected to terminal 1), tone cap C1 shunts highs to ground. As you turn the control progressively more clockwise, the tone becomes brighter, just like a standard tone control. But in the last few degrees of rotation, the coil tap connects to ground, thus (in the case of a humbucker) giving a bright, single coil sound, and in the case of a tapped single coil pickup, giving a thinner, more "vintage" sound.

I can't recommend this circuit highly enough. If you also have an in-phase/out-of-phase switch, the number of possible tone combinations is amazing—and they're all musically useful.

YOUR CORD IS A TONE CONTROL

The type of cord you use can make a substantial difference in your overall sound. With a shielded cable, the hot lead and shield interact and create a small amount of capacitance, since the shield connects to ground, just as with a standard tone control there's a capacitor shunting highs from the audio line to ground. Granted this is a small amount of capacitance compared to a tone control's capacitor, but it can nonetheless affect your sound.

I ran some tests and found that coil cords tend to have the greatest amount of cable capacitance. If you're using one, switch over to a standard cord and you'll probably notice an improved high end. Unfortunately, even very low-capacitance cables may dull your sound a bit if you have a relatively long cord trailing back to your amp. In a case like this, building a small buffer board or preamp into your guitar can isolate your axe from the "loading" effects of the cord, and deliver a cleaner, brighter, more hum-free signal to your amp. This book presents four possible solutions: Project #7, Buffer Board (simplest), Project #8, Clarifier (includes tone controls), and Project #9 IGGY (can also drive balanced lines in the studio). If you're really ambitious, check out Project #31, Design An On-Board Guitar Preamp, in Chapter 10.

Taken as a group, the above tips can really make a big difference in your guitar sound—don't think that just because they're extremely simple, they're not worth trying.

✳ PROJECT 17 HUMBUCKING PICKUP TRICKS

Lurking deep within your humbucking pickups are a whole bunch of sounds that can be yours for a little bit of time and rewiring.

A humbucking pickup consists of two single coil pickups, connected in series and electrically out of phase with each other (Fig. 6-6). Note that although the coils are electrically out of phase to cancel hum, according to DiMarzio's Steve Blucher in an audio sense they produce an additive effect.

However, these coils don't have to be connected in this way, which is the secret to getting a bunch of alternate sounds; they can be wired in phase, in parallel, or one coil can even be ignored entirely for more of a single coil sound. Let's look at some possibilities, along with subjective evaluations of the sounds produced by different rewirings.

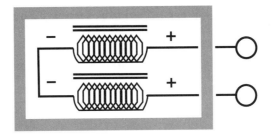

**Fig. 6-6
Standard humbucker
wiring, with two
coils wired in series
and electrically out
of phase.**

BUT FIRST,
A WORD OF CAUTION

Before you embark on rewiring, note that some replacement pickups make the four terminals (two for each coil) easily accessible. Other pickups, especially older types, will require micro-surgery to isolate the four coil connections. Pickup wires are delicate; do not attempt pickup rewirings unless you are well-versed in electronic construction techniques.

Incidentally, if you want to access all possible pickup combinations, your guitar will grow a forest of toggle switches that will make it harder to find your sound. I recommend you not experiment on something like a vintage Les Paul. Instead, practice on a less-than-wonderful guitar and try out all the various options. Some will sound better to you than others; either permanently wire your pickup the way you like it, or if a few different wirings appeal to you, work out a switching scheme that provides your favorite sounds. You may want to replace some pots with versions having integral push/pull switches, as these can provide switching options without your having to drill new holes in your axe.

Ready? Let's go.

SERIES VS. PARALLEL

First, let's look at the difference between series and parallel connections. Fig. 6-7 shows two coils in series; Fig. 6-8 shows two coils in parallel. Each configuration gives a distinctive sound. Series connections can give more output and produce a "heavier" sound. However, this increases the pickup's output impedance, so the guitar should feed circuits with very high input impedances. (For why this is important, see Project 28, Testing Impedance.)

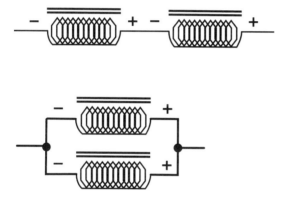

Fig. 6-7
Two pickup coils connected in series.

Fig. 6-8
Two pickup coils connected in parallel.

HUMBUCKING WIRING OPTIONS

Fig. 6-9 shows a humbucker wired with the coils in series, but this time, the coils are in phase; in other words, one coil's (+) feeds the other coil's (-). This drops the output considerably and gives a "thin," out-of-phase sound. You also lose the hum canceling properties (but that's a limitation of all these rewirings; there's no free lunch, right?).

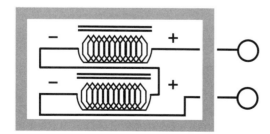

Fig. 6-9
Pickup coils wired in series, and in phase, give a thin output.

Fig. 6-10

Pickup coils wired in parallel and in phase.

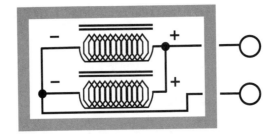

Fig. 6-10
Pickup coils wired in
parallel and in
phase.

In Fig. 6-10, the two coils are in parallel and in phase with each other. This creates slightly less output than the series configuration in Fig. 6-6, but the highs are somewhat more defined—especially if your guitar is feeding a circuit with a relatively low input impedance.

Fig. 6-11 connects both coils in parallel, but out of phase. This produces an almost complete cancellation of the sound coming out of the pickup. The tone is very thin and low-level, but changing the pole piece screws of one of the coils to place them closer to the strings can provide a little more juice.

For a single coil sound, wire up just one coil or the other (Fig. 6-12). Generally you'll want to choose the coil with the exposed pole pieces if only one set is visible.

Fig. 6-11
Wiring pickup coils
in parallel but out of
phase almost
completely cancels
the sound.

Fig. 6-12
Imitating a single
coil sound with a
humbucker.

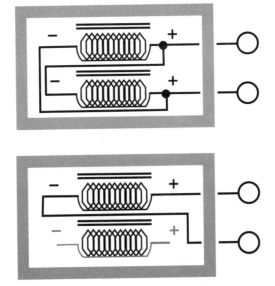

IS REWIRING WORTH THE EFFORT?

The process of experimenting with sound is always fun, but we're talking about a fair amount of work here. If you like the sound of your stock guitar, then "if it ain't broke, don't fix it." But some of these variations are really quite useful; in particular, the "single coil" option adds a whole different tonal quality.

✳ *PROJECT* **18**
POTS AND PANS

There's more than one way to switch pickups—and this method doesn't involve a switch at all, but a panpot that gives a continuously variable sweep between two pickups.

A pickup selector switch is a good way to change sounds fast, but you can obtain all kinds of interesting and subtle shadings if you use a panpot instead. This control pans between treble and bass pickups, like the way a mixer panpot sweeps between the left and right channels. If you'd like a wider range of colors from your axe without resorting to outboard boxes such as equalizers, this circuit may be just what the doctor ordered.

ADVANTAGES AND DISADVANTAGES

With a three-way pickup selector switch, there are no ambiguous positions: you have bass, treble, or both pickups—period. A panpot control has two unambiguous positions at the extremes of rotation, but there's a whole range of possible sounds in between those two extremes. These variations are subtle, but usable; they're particularly effective if an additional tone control circuit provides further variations. So, the basic tradeoff is that it's more difficult to dial in an exact setting than with a standard pickup selector switch, but you get more possibilities in return.

CONSTRUCTION STRATEGIES

This circuit uses one dual-ganged potentiometer, a standard potentiometer, and an SPDT (single pole, double throw) switch that includes a third, *center-off* position. This combination of controls means that if your guitar has a selector switch/volume/

tone control combination, you can retrofit for panning with no extra holes required (however, using a dual pot—which is deeper than a single pot—may be a problem for some guitars).

There are a lot of variables in this circuit, so I'd suggest temporarily running a pair of wires (hot and ground) from each pickup to a test jig where you can experiment with different parts values. After all, one important reason for doing it yourself is so you can get exactly what *you* want to hear. Once you find the sound you like, build the circuitry inside the guitar. By the way, as you test make sure the metal cases of any pots or switches are grounded, or you'll have hum problems.

HOW IT WORKS

Dual-ganged panpot R3 is the heart of the circuit (Fig. 6-13). A true panpot usually has a *log* taper for one element and an *antilog* taper for the other element because this gives the best "feel" and most even panning response (we don't need to explain why, just take my word for it). Log/antilog taper pots are very rare, but there's a workaround: use an ordinary dual-ganged *linear taper* pot and add "tapering" resistors R1 and R2. These should equal 20% of the pot's total resistance; adding them as shown changes the pot taper to a log/antilog curve.

Higher resistance values generally provide a crisper, more accurate high end but the circuit will be more susceptible to

Fig. 6-13
Pickup panpot
schematic.

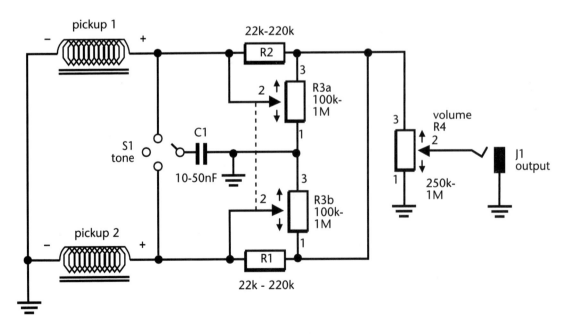

noise and hum. Lower values can result in a quieter circuit but may also reduce the highs and output somewhat. The latter could actually be a benefit if you play through distortion, though, since a reduced high end will tend to warm the sound up a bit. I'd recommend a range of values for the panpot between 100k and 1 Meg (these would require 22k and 220k tapering resistors respectively). Note, however, that a 100k panpot with 22k tapering resistors will cause noticeable dulling and a loss of volume *unless* you use active pickups (like EMGs). In that case, lower resistor values are preferred to higher values.

Volume control R4 can be a 250K, 500K, or 1 Meg log (audio) taper control.

The tone control was designed specifically for this circuit. S1 connects capacitor C1 across one pickup, the other pickup, or neither pickup (the tone switch's center position); the capacitor shunts high frequencies to ground, which reduces the highs. I was surprised at how switching in the capacitor can change the timbre at the panpot's mid position, and this definitely multiplies the number of tonal options. The capacitor value is a matter of taste, but a good range is from 0.01µF (10nF) for a little bit of high-end dulling to 0.05µF (50nF) for a bassier sound.

Note that you could also use different capacitor values for the two pickups if you connect the switch's center terminal to ground, and run a capacitor from each switch terminal to its corresponding pickup.

TWEAKS

It's important to adjust the two pickups for the same relative output; use the screw adjustments on the side of the pickup assemblies. If one pickup predominates, it will shift the panpot's apparent center.

If you want an additional set of sounds, switching one of the pickups out-of-phase (in other words, reversing the + and - connections) gives some useful effects. Also note that removing the tapering resistors may produce a feel that you prefer, particularly if one of the pickups is out of phase.

This type of circuit can also be very effective on bass, but to tune it down an octave you'll need to double the tone control capacitor values.

That's about it…and you don't even need batteries!

PARTS LIST

Resistors   (1/4 watt, 5% or 10% tolerance except as noted)

R1, R2   22k-220k (see text)

R3   Dual ganged panpot, 100k-1M (see text)

R4   250k-1M (see text)

Capacitors (10 working volts or greater)

C1   0.01µF-0.05µF (10nF-50nF, see text)

Other parts

S1   SPDT center-off switch

J1   Mono, open circuit, ¼" phone jack

Misc.   Wire, solder, knob, etc.

✴ PROJECT 19
TELECASTER REWIRING

To heat up your axe with some totally tantalizing tones, check out this simple guitar rewiring—and add a bunch of new sounds for very little bucks.

The rewiring shown in Fig. 6-14 is designed specifically for Telecasters and Tele "clones" (however, the same principles apply to rewiring any dual-pickup guitar). Retrofitting the stock 3-way switch with a 5-way replacement gives two extra pickup switching options, and you can also add a phase switch for two additional sounds. None of this requires modifying the body.

THE SHIELD BLUES

With many pickups, there are two leads, hot and ground. The ground lead often connects to a metal shield or casing around the pickup. Reversing the pickup leads to switch the phase can make the metal shield "hot," so not only does it *not* shield, it actually acts as an antenna for signals and hum.

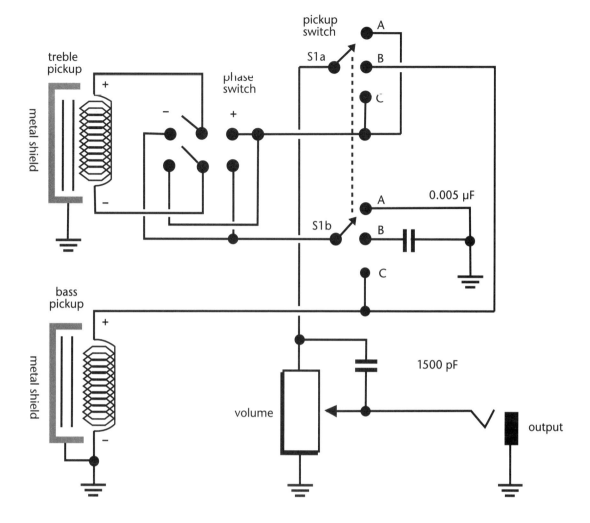

Fig. 6-14
Hot rod Telecaster
rewiring.

The solution: disconnect the pickup ground wire from the casing, and treat it as the pickup's (-) lead (as indicated on the schematic). Then, run a lead from the casing itself to any convenient ground point, such as the ground lug on the volume control or output jack.

THE BIG SWITCH

Stock Teles have three-position selector switches for selecting among bass (neck), treble (bridge), and both pickups. 2-pole, 5-way Strat switches, offered as replacement parts that fit in the same sized slot as the regular switch, have two more positions since they can "short out" the intermediary positions between the three main settings.

When I did this rewiring to my Tele, I wanted to avoid drilling any holes in the guitar. So, I removed the tone control and replaced it with a DPDT switch for the phase flip function. Since I still wanted a mellow bass sound available, the fourth pickup switch position puts a tone control capacitor across the signal line, just like a tone control set to full on. The fifth position puts the two pickups in series for a hotter sound.

The pickup switch options are:

Position A: Treble pickup only
Position A+B: Treble and bass pickup in parallel
Position B: Bass pickup only
Position B+C: Bass pickup with tone control capacitor
Position C: Treble and bass pickups in series

The phase switch flips the treble pickup wires before they go to the pickup selector, but the phase change only affects dual-pickup configurations (switch positions A+B and C).

The 0.005μF (5nF) capacitor is the "tone control" capacitor. The higher the value, the more high frequencies it rolls off, and the mellower the sound. Try 0.01μF (10nF), or even 0.022μF (22nF) for a really deep tone.

The 1500pF (1n5) capacitor increases the amount of high frequencies as you turn down the volume control, thus giving a brighter sound for rhythm parts. Smaller values have less of an effect. This circuit is very useful for distortion—turn the volume down a little bit and the tone gets a lot more biting, with less bottom.

There's not much else to the mod except for the usual cautions: if you don't know what you're doing, don't do it! You wouldn't want to ruin a stock guitar finish by splashing solder on it. Other than that, enjoy your new sounds.

Projects for the Studio

✳ PROJECT **20**
BALANCED/UNBALANCED ADAPTER

When making the transition from guitar boxes to studio effects, sometimes "you can't get there from here" due to connector mismatches. This quick and dirty little adapter box solves the problem.

Most guitar effects are designed with two-wire, unbalanced inputs and outputs that have a "hot" and ground connection. However, in the studio a lot of high-end gear uses three-wire, balanced inputs and outputs with "hot," "cold," and ground lines. When you need to hook an unbalanced and balanced line

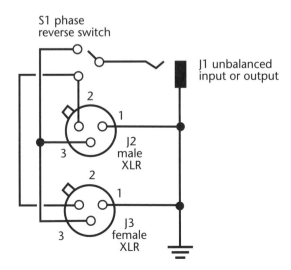

S1 phase
reverse switch

J1 unbalanced
input or output

2
1
3
J2
male
XLR

2
1
3
J3
female
XLR

Fig. 7-1
Unbalanced-to-balanced line adapter.

together, what are you gonna do? Build the Balanced/Unbalanced Adapter.

CONSTRUCTION TIPS

The adapter (Fig. 7-1) is pretty simple, and lends itself to mounting in a small aluminum box. Drill holes for the connectors and switch, then wire them up.

USING THE BALANCED/UNBALANCED ADAPTER

You can't get much simpler than this. Patch the unbalanced line into J1. Patch the balanced line into J2 or J3, depending on which interfaces with your particular patch cable or adapter.

Phase reverse switch S1 accommodates those manufacturers who are not yet aware that there's an international standard, IEC 268, that specifies pin 2 of an XLR connector as being the "hot" signal pin, and instead wire pin 3 as hot.

We should mention that this is a very basic way of doing an adapter, and that if you're converting an unbalanced line to a balanced line, it doesn't take advantage of the features a balanced line system offers. Nor can you drive a balanced line input directly from a guitar with non-active pickups, since the loading will suck all the sound out of your axe. If you want to feed a balanced line in style, check out the next project (Direct Injector) or Project #9, IGGY line driver. But when you "can't get there from here," this simple project could be a session-saver.

PARTS LIST

J1	Mono, open circuit, ¼" phone jack
J2	3-pin male XLR connector
J3	3-pin female XLR connector
S1	SPDT switch

✳ PROJECT 21
THE DIRECT INJECTOR

In the studio, there are several advantages to "going direct" into a mixing console or effects unit instead of using a microphone: less noise, less distortion, and a clearer sound. But to gain the maximum benefits from this approach, you need a direct box designed specifically for guitar—and that's what the Direct Injector is all about.

If you record guitar in the studio, here's the direct box for you. Optimized for guitar, bass, and Chapman Stick, the Direct Injector:

- Matches these instruments (as well as guitar-level signal processors) to pro-style balanced gear

- Buffers them from the loading effects of long cable runs or signal processors/amps with low impedance inputs, thus improving clarity and reducing muddiness

- Mixes stereo instruments to mono

- Delivers 6-24 dB of gain

- Has CD-quality noise specs

    ...and it's not too hard to build, either (Fig. 7-2).

> **Fig. 7-2**
> **Direct Injector schematic.**

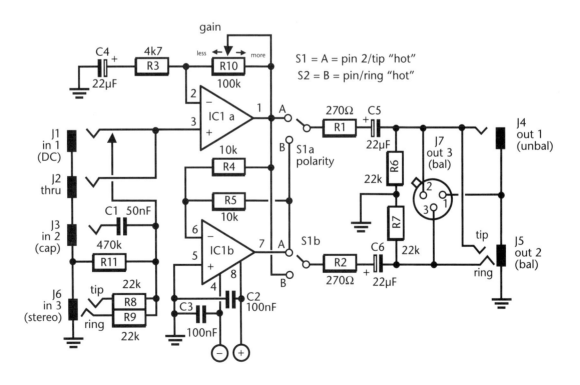

INPUTS, OUTPUTS, CONTROLS

Input J1 is almost always the best input to use but if you experience problems with some active electronics or signal processor outputs, try J3. J6 is for stereo instruments *(e.g.,* Chapman Stick); it mixes the two signals into a mono output. J2 carries the same signal present at J1, J3, or J6. Use this to split the instrument signal to a tuner, amplifier, etc.

J4 provides an unbalanced ¼" phone output, J5 a balanced ¼" phone output, and J7 a balanced XLR connector output.

There are two controls. R10 (Gain) sets gain from X1 to X20. S1 (Polarity) chooses whether XLR pin 2 and the ¼" phone tip, or XLR pin 3 and the ¼" phone ring, carry the "hot" signals.

HOW IT WORKS

IC1a provides the amplified, non-inverting ("hot") signal and also feeds unity gain inverting amp IC1b, which generates the inverting ("cold") signal. S1 routes the two op amp outputs to the output connectors differently, depending on which polarity you select.

Regarding the inputs, J3 provides traditional capacitive coupling and a discharge path to ground (R11). R11's high resistance avoids loading down an instrument's sensitive pickups, but unfortunately, higher resistance leads to more noise.

Plugging a guitar into J1 improves the noise performance, especially if the instrument's volume control is up full. In this case, the op amp "sees" a low resistance path to ground through the pickup wiring, which reduces noise; meanwhile, the pickup "sees" the op amp's high input impedance. The result: very little loading *and* very low noise. The NE5532 (IC1) is a dual op amp that features high slew rate, quiet operation, and the ability to drive 600Ω lines.

FINDING PARTS

Except for the NE5532, all parts are relatively common and available at stores such as Radio Shack. The power supply can be any well-filtered, bipolar, DC power supply between ±9 and ±18 volts (more volts gives more headroom), such as the AC Power Supply (Project #12) presented in this book. You can even use two pairs of 9V batteries (wired in series) if hum is a problem, or to help avoid shock hazard. However, batteries are the least environmentally sound power option.

CONSTRUCTION

Route the input and output wires away from each other. The leads going to J1-J3 and J6, as well as connections to IC pins 2 and 6, should be as short as possible. I'd recommend mounting the Direct Injector in a rack mount enclosure, but if you use a plastic case, R10's case must connect to ground.

Speaking of ground, the connections from IC1b pin 5, the junctions of R6/R7 and C2/C3, and pin 1 of XLR connector J7 should connect directly to J1's ground connection. J7's shield pin (pin 4, not shown) can connect to any chassis ground point.

MODIFICATIONS

If you experience RFI (Radio Frequency Interference), connect a low value (10pF or so) capacitor from IC1a pin 3 to ground. Also, note that pin 3 has no protection other than what's inside the chip. If you're paranoid about static electricity, insert a 1k resistor between IC1a pin 3 and the line going to the various input jacks.

To double the available gain (but also the potential for more noise and clipping distortion), change R3 to 2.2k (2k2).

USING IT

The Direct Injector is well-suited to driving any kind of balanced input *(e.g.,* pro signal processor or console) from an unbalanced output. Choose the right kind of input and output connector, adjust the Polarity switch as needed, and set the gain for the desired kick.

Important: Don't overlook using the unbalanced output (J4) to drive studio-oriented signal processors that, even though they have a ¼" phone jack input, load down pickups due to a low input impedance (even some guitar boxes do this). Using the

Direct Injector to provide proper matching between the guitar and processor can greatly increase the guitar's "sparkle."

And that's about all there is to it. Happy recording, and may you never hear a muddy, mismatched guitar, bass, or Stick sound again.

SPECIFICATIONS

Frequency response: ±0.2 dB, 20 Hz-80 kHz

Signal-to-noise ratio (unweighted, 6 dB gain, output 1): -102 dB

Signal-to-noise ratio (unweighted, 6 dB gain, output 2): -96 dB

Signal-to-noise ratio (unweighted, 24 dB gain): better than -88 dB

Input impedance, J3: >400kΩ

Input impedance, J1: >1 MegΩ

Output impedance: 600Ω

Max headroom (±15V power supply): >26V peak to peak

Gain range: 6 dB to 24 dB

PARTS LIST

Resistors	(5% tolerance, metal film preferred for fixed resistors)
R1, R2	270Ω
R3	4.7k (4k7)
R4, R5	10k
R6-R9	22k
R10	100k linear taper pot
R11	470k
Capacitors	(50 or more working volts, mylar or polystyrene preferred except as noted)
C1	0.05µF (50nF)
C2, C3	0.1µF (100nF)
C4-C6	22µF, tantalum or electrolytic
Jacks	
J1	Mono, open circuit, ¼" switching phone jack
J2-J4	Mono, open circuit, ¼" phone jacks
J5-J6	Stereo, open circuit, ¼" phone jacks
J7	Female XLR connector
Other parts	
IC1	NE5532 or equivalent (see text)
S1	2-pole, 2-position toggle switch
Misc.	IC socket, perfboard, wire, socket, knob, power supply, etc.

✻ PROJECT 22
TAPE RECORDER TO ECHO UNIT CONVERSION

Some musicians still prefer the "softer" sound of tape echo units over the "harsher" sound of digital delay, even though the latter is more flexible and convenient. Although echo units based on tape are an endangered species, here's how to get the same kind of sound out of an analog tape recorder.

Now that digital media such as DAT (Digital Audio Tape) have become a mainstay in most studios for 2-track mixes, there are a lot of half-track and quarter-track reel-to-reel tape recorders sitting around gathering dust. This project tells how to turn those recorders into productive citizens once more, by converting them into an echo unit with a smooth "analog sound" that distorts much more sweetly than digital delays.

ANALOG VS. DIGITAL ECHO

Although tape echo may seem anachronistic, sound is the bottom line and if an older piece of equipment does the job, there's no reason not to use it (just think of all the recording studios that pay gobs of money for vintage tube equipment). Another advantage of using tape is that if you hit it with a lot of level, the sound doesn't "splatter" as with a digital delay, but instead acquires a powerful, somewhat bigger sound.

Although tape echo units are getting hard to find, for those instances where you want a true tape echo sound any three-head reel-to-reel (or even three-head analog cassette) deck will do the job. Older models can often be picked up secondhand for under $100. Of course, there are disadvantages to using a tape recorder as an echo unit instead of a digital delay; your choice of delay times is more limited (although a recorder with variable speed helps), it will not be possible to obtain short delays (as required for flanging and chorusing), and you can't add modulation. So I'm certainly not saying that tape echo is inherently better than digital, but if you're looking for a vintage echo sound, it's the only way to go.

HOOKING IT UP

In addition to the tape recorder, you will need some other submodules. Referring to Fig. 7-3, there are two mixers and a buffer/preamp (this stage prevents the mixer inputs from loading down the guitar). The buffer could be a preamp, compressor, etc.

Just about anything that mixes two inputs into a single output will work for the mixers. Several companies make mini-mixers that will do the job, or you could build project #18 from the book *Electronic Projects for Musicians* (published by AMSCO).

You will probably need some adapter cords to connect the mixers (which usually have ¼" phone jacks) to the tape recorder (which usually has RCA phono jacks), and you will also need two "Y" cords as indicated.

USING THE TAPE ECHO UNIT

The controls need to be set carefully for best results—specifically, you may need to "tweak" things a bit to match levels between the guitar, mixers, and recorder. Start by turning up Mixer 1, Channel 2 and Mixer 2, Channel 2 full blast; turning down Mixer 1, Channel 1 and Mixer 2, Channel 1; and listening to the output of Mixer 2. As you play, you should hear your normal guitar sound at its normal level.

Fig. 7-3
Hookup diagram for turning a tape recorder into an echo unit.

Now thread some tape on to the recorder, push the record and play buttons to start recording, and make sure that the recorder's output monitors the playback head. (Remember, the recorder must have a separate playback head for this technique to work.)

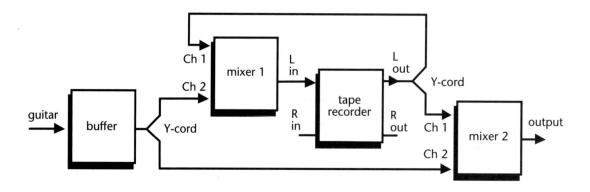

Turn up the recorder's input level control so that the guitar signal starts registering on the recorder's VU meters. Once you've set a good recording level, turn up Mixer 2, Channel 1 to add the echoed sound in with the straight guitar sound. If you don't hear any delayed sound, check that the tape is running, the recorder is in record mode, you are monitoring from the play head, and that all patch cords are hooked up correctly.

So far you should be hearing only one repeat. To increase the number of repeats, turn up Mixer 1, Channel 1. This takes some of the recorder output and feeds it back into the input, thus creating a feedback loop. Careful, though; if you turn this control up too far you'll get runaway feedback.

Note that when you run out of tape, you run out of echo. Be sure to rewind the tape periodically.

FURTHER REFINEMENTS

You can change the echo time by changing the recorder's speed; a variable speed recorder gives more options. Also, don't forget that with a stereo recorder, you have two channels to mess with—you can even patch the two channels in series and select the slowest tape speed possible for super-long echoes. Or, feed both channels simultaneously and send the recorder outputs to different stereo channels.

If you want whisper-quiet echo effects, add noise reduction to the tape recorder. When using something like dbx noise reduction, you would encode the signal coming from Mixer 1 going into the recorder, and decode the signal coming from the tape recorder before it hits the Y-cord. This can improve the signal-to-noise ratio by up to 30 dB.

That's just about all there is to it. The next time you know someone who wants to junk an old 3-head reel-to-reel recorder, ask if you can have it. Clean and demagnetize the heads, dust out the insides, do a little maintenance, and add the support circuitry mentioned in this project; the result will be a vintage tape echo unit sound for a minimal cash outlay.

Vintage Effects Helpers

✳ PROJECT 23
BUILDING A BETTER BYPASS

Vintage effects can make some very cool sounds when active, but degrade your sound when bypassed. Fortunately, there's a solution—and a simple one at that.

You've read the tips on restoring vintage effects (Project #24), and finally, your Super Mindmelt Psycho-Flanger is ready for action. You plug in your guitar, and—yes! It's that classic 70s sound that inspired millions to exclaim "wow, man." Flushed with artistic fulfillment, you return to your straight guitar sound for a bit and...

It sounds like garbage. So why is your beloved Psycho-Flanger trashing the *straight* guitar sound? Let's find out, then fix the problem once and for all.

GETTING LOADED

A guitar with passive pickups produces a weak signal that can get loaded down by subsequent effects circuitry (unless it's carefully designed, which was rare in the old days). Loading decreases the signal level and often reduces high frequencies.

If you're bonged out of your mind and going through a stack o' amps running at 120% distortion, you might not notice

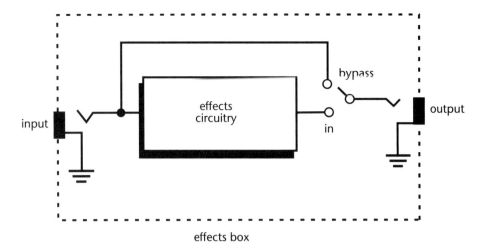

effects box

the difference. But if you care about a guitar's natural sound as well as its processed one, getting rid of loading can give your sound a lot more level and presence.

With many vintage effects, the bypass switch design is the main culprit. To save a few bucks, manufacturers would use an inexpensive single-pole, double-throw (SPDT) bypass switch to choose between the processed and dry sounds (Fig. 8-1). However, in the bypass (dry) position, your guitar still feeds the effect electronics, which can load down your axe and suck signal from it. It's like what happens to your car when you drive with the parking brake on.

Fig. 8-1
Cheapo effects bypass method using SPDT switch.

THE BIG FIX

Upscale vintage effects often used a double-pole, double-throw (DPDT) switch (Fig. 8-2). This type of switch contains two linked SPDT switches in a single housing, which provides independent

Fig. 8-2
Better bypassing using DPDT switch.

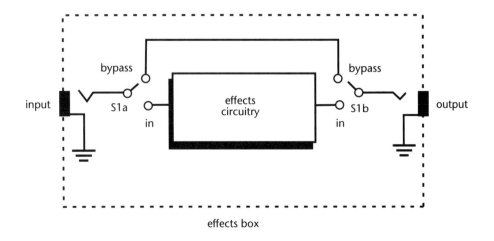

effects box

switching of the effect's input *and* output. Now when you bypass the effect, the guitar signal has a straight shot to the output jack and doesn't get distracted by the effects circuitry.

If you can solder, know electronics, and don't mind decimating the resale value of your vintage effect, you can replace the SPDT switch with a DPDT type. However, there's a better option: build a "universal" true bypass box that works with any effect.

BE TRUE TO YOUR BYPASS

You can build the true bypass box (Fig. 8-3) in an evening. It requires only four jacks, two resistors, metal case, and DPDT footswitch. Note that you may need to reinforce consumer-style cases, which usually aren't built with footswitch stomping in mind.

All parts except the footswitch are commonly available from electronics suppliers; you can order a suitable footswitch from Stewart-McDonald's Guitar Shop Supply (tel. 800/848-2273).

To build the box, first drill holes for the four jacks and footswitch, then install these parts in the case. Next, mount the two resistors between the hot and ground tabs of their associated jacks, then use point-to-point wiring to complete all the connections. Make sure that nothing shorts out to the case cover when you close things back up.

Operation is simple. Patch your guitar into the input jack, and your amp into the output. Patch the effect input to the "to

**Fig. 8-3
Universal, true
bypass switching
box.**

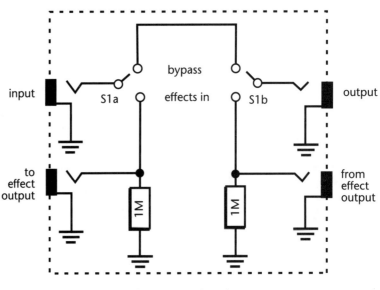

true bypass switching box

DO-IT-YOURSELF PROJECTS FOR GUITARISTS

effect input" jack, and the effect output to the "to effect output" jack. Leave the effect in the active position at all times; do all in/out switching at the true bypass box.

The resistors aren't always necessary, but they do minimize the chance of an effect "popping" when you switch in and out (this can happen with effects that use a particular "save-a-few-cents" input stage configuration).

Even some newer effects can benefit from the true bypass box. Although recent designs tend not to load down your guitar as much, they often process your signal through active electronics at all times. Using the true bypass box guarantees a straight wire between your guitar and amp (or subsequent effect).

There, that wasn't too difficult. Now you can really enjoy your Super Mindmelt Psycho-Flanger—even when it's bypassed.

PARTS LIST

2	1 Meg resistors
4	Mono, open circuit, ¼" phone jacks
1	DPDT footswitch (see text)
Misc.	Case, hardware, solder, wire, etc.

✳ PROJECT 24
RESTORING VINTAGE EFFECTS

So you finally tracked down an ultra-rare, ultra-retro Phase Warper stomp box. Unfortunately, it's not working quite right; sitting unused in someone's garage has taken its toll. But if you apply a few basic procedures, you can often nurse that antique back to life.

Even if you're not too much into do-it-yourself, restoring a vintage effect is not too difficult a task—some cleaning, tightening, and a little contact cleaner can result in a unit that's as good as new. However, there are a few important cautions when doing any kind of repair job:

■ When you disassemble the unit, don't lose any mounting screws. Keep a small cup around and put the screws in there.

- If a unit seems difficult to disassemble, don't force things. Sometimes a screw will be hidden under a sticker, or will be accessible only if you remove a knob or panel. Another place to look for screws is in the battery compartment once you've removed the batteries.

- Proceed very, very cautiously when disassembling a unit. Take all the time in the world, because you don't want the cure to be worse than the disease. If your screwdriver slips and you destroy some part that was discontinued in 1972, you'll be very sorry.

With these cautions out of the way, let's get specific.

BLOW IT AWAY

Older effects often come with large amounts of dust. Get a can of compressed air, take the unit outside, and blow air on the effect to get rid of as much dust as possible. In a pinch, you can plug a vacuum cleaner's hose into the exhaust end, let the vacuum run for a minute or so to clear out any dust stuck in the hose, then clean out the effect. Now you're ready to get to work.

SOME EFFECTS HAVE A SCREW LOOSE

Enough vibration can loosen screws, causing bad ground connections (vintage effects sometimes depend on mounting screws to provide an electrical path between circuit board and ground, or panel and ground).

While you still have the unit apart, try to turn each screw (except those that regulate something, such as trimpots) to see if there's any play. If so, tighten the nut and if there isn't already a lockwasher, add one underneath the nut. Be careful not to overtighten.

Also check the condition of the line cord or AC adapter jack. Replace it if you have any doubts about its ability to carry power safely.

SPRAY YOUR WAY
TO REPAIRS

One of the biggest problems is oxidation, which coats metal surfaces with an insulating film or corrosion due to stuff in the air (whether pollution in L.A. or salt spray in Maine). This can cause scratchy sounds in pots, intermittent problems with switches, and even occasional circuit malfunctions. Fortunately, chemicals called contact cleaners can solve a lot of these problems. I've had good luck with DeoxIT from Caig Laboratories, but there are many other types (such as "Blue Shower" contact cleaner). Here are some typical contact cleaner applications:

- **Scratchy pots.** Pots use a metal wiper that rubs across a resistive strip; if oxidation or film prevents these from making contact, the pot becomes an intermittent open circuit. To solve this, spray a small amount of contact cleaner into the pot's case. With unsealed rotary pots, there's usually an opening next to the pot's terminals. Slide pots have an obvious opening. Sealed pots are more difficult to spray; sometimes the pot can be disassembled, sprayed, and reassembled. Or, dribble contact cleaner down the side of the pot's shaft, and hope some of it makes it to the innards.

  Once sprayed, you have to rotate the pot several times to "smear" the cleaner, and flush away the gunk it's dissolving. After rotating about a dozen times, spray in a *little* more contact cleaner and rotate a dozen more times.

  If the problem returns later, spray and rotate again. However, remember that eventually a pot's resistive element becomes so worn that no contact cleaner can restore it. You then need to replace the pot with one of equivalent value.

  Incidentally, people often forget that trimpots need cleaning too—especially since they're more exposed than regular pots. The main caution here is that the trimpot setting may be critical, so take careful note of where it was set. The best way to do this is to measure the voltage at the trimpot's wiper, and after cleaning, set the trimpot to produce the same wiper voltage. (If there's no voltage reading, measure the resistance between the wiper and another terminal, and duplicate that.)

- **IC sockets.** IC sockets can also oxidize. A quick fix is to use a spring steel IC extractor (about $3) to pull up slightly on the chip (just enough to loosen it—about $\frac{1}{16}$"). Apply a tiny bit of contact cleaner to each of the IC pins. Now push the IC back into its socket. The scraping of the chip pins against the socket in conjunction with the cleaner should clean things enough to make good electrical contact. If not, try again. *Caution!* IC pins are fragile, so don't pull the chip out too far, or perform this procedure too often.

- **Unsealed rotary and pushbutton switches.** These respond well to contact cleaners, but toggle switches are often sealed. These are usually not worth disassembling; replacement is your best bet.

- **Other connectors.** Connector pins in general can develop oxidation, and are candidates for spraying.

- **Battery connectors.** Since these connectors carry the most current of anything in the effect, oxidation here can be a real problem. Spray the connector, and snap/unsnap the battery several times.

    Two other battery tips: Check the battery connector tabs that mate with the battery's positive terminal. If they don't make good contact, push inward on the connector tabs with a pliers or screwdriver to encourage firmer contact. And if the battery has leaked on the connector, don't try to salvage it—solder in a new connector.

THOSE #@$$#^ FOOTSWITCHES

Many old stomp boxes use push-on, push-off DPDT footswitches that are expensive and difficult to find. One source for replacements is Stewart-McDonald's Guitar Shop Supply (800/848-2273).

YOU DON'T MISS
YOUR ELECTROLYTE UNTIL
THE WELL RUNS DRY

Electrolytic capacitors contain a chemical that dries up over time. With very old effects, or ones that have been subject to environmental extremes *(e.g.,* being on the road with a rock and roll band), replacing old electrolytic capacitors with newer ones of the same value and voltage rating can improve the sound. Note that ceramic capacitors (usually disc-shaped) and tantalum caps (like electrolytics, but generally smaller for a given value and with a lower voltage rating) don't dry out.

SAFER POWER

Many older AC-powered boxes did not use fuses or three-conductor AC cords. Although you don't want to modify a vintage box too much, making a concession to safety is a different matter. The schematic in Fig. 8-4 shows how to convert a two-wire cord to a fused, three-wire type. *Caution: This mod involves use of AC. Unless you are experienced with electronics technology and the precautions needed with lethal voltages, have a qualified technician do this mod.*

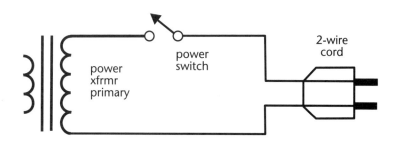

Fig. 8-4
Converting a two-wire AC cord to a three-wire type.

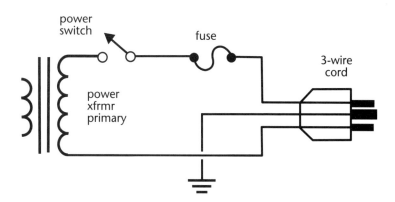

The 3-wire cord's ground should connect to the effect's main ground point (usually the chassis). The fuse can be an in-line type so that it fits in the effect case (make sure any AC wiring you add is *extremely* well-insulated from the case). Use a fuse with a current rating about 1.2 times the effect's current rating.

GOOD LUCK...

Your toughest task in restoring vintage effects will be finding obsolete parts such as old analog delay chips, custom-made optoisolators, and dealing with effects where they sanded off the IC identification (a primitive form of copy protection). But once you restore an effect, it's a great feeling…and you know, sometimes they really do sound better.

✳ *PROJECT* 25
VINTAGE EFFECTS DE-HISSER

Nothing can replace the sound of vintage effects, but the digital era has spoiled us: older effects often suffer from noise levels that sound very out of place on a CD or DAT. Dolby or dbx noise reduction is one option, but here's a far less expensive alternative that still gives pretty good results.

Fig. 8-5
The De-Hisser pre-emphasis section boosts treble going into the effect.

The De-Hisser is based on a very old type of noise reduction that uses pre-emphasis (treble boosting) and de-emphasis (complementary treble-cutting). By using the circuit in Fig. 8-5 to

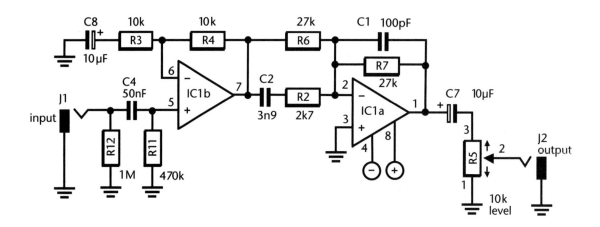

DO-IT-YOURSELF PROJECTS FOR GUITARISTS

boost the treble of the signal going into the effect, the sound going through the effect is unnaturally "bright."

After exiting the effect, the signal passes through a de-emphasis circuit (Fig. 8-6), which cuts the treble by an equal amount to restore the timbre of the original signal. Perhaps more importantly, since hiss is most objectionable at high frequencies, the treble-cutting action also reduces the apparent amount of hiss coming out of the device.

Fig. 8-6
The De-Hisser de-emphasis circuit cuts treble by an amount equal to the pre-emphasis boost.

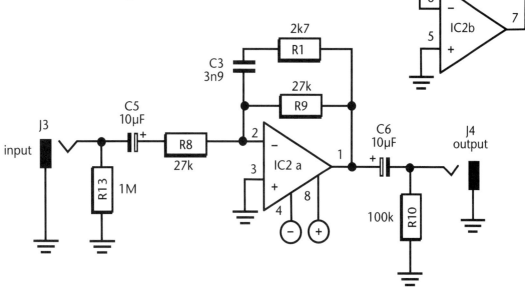

Your guitar plugs into J1. IC1a is a simple buffer that converts the guitar output into a low impedance signal capable of driving pre-emphasis filter IC1b. The pre-emphasized output appears at J2, and patches to the effect's input. The signal returning from the effect plugs into J3. IC2a is the de-emphasis circuit; this output couples through C6 and appears at J4.

If you're using several effects in series, try using the pre-emphasis filter at the beginning of the chain, and the de-emphasis filter at the end.

CONSTRUCTION TIPS

This circuit requires a bipolar power supply, which can be anywhere in the range of ±5V to ±15V. Thus, battery power is acceptable, as is the AC Power Supply (Project #12). If you are using batteries, unplug them when not in use or add a DPST or DPDT on-off power switch. For more information on how to switch two batteries on and off, see the Buffer Board (Project #7).

Building the De-Hisser is not critical, except that you must use good quality polystyrene or mylar capacitors for C2 and C3. Also note that we've specified two dual op amps, but are only using three op amps. The fourth op amp should be disabled as shown in Fig. 8-6, so that it doesn't oscillate or cause other problems. You can use op amps other than the 5532 (such as the 5558, which is common but noisy), or three individual op amps (such as three LF351 ICs); however, the pinout may not be the same as the one indicated on the schematic. If you use other op amps, consult manufacturer's data books for their pinouts, and make sure you connect all power and ground lines properly.

USING THE DE-HISSER

Plug in as described earlier, and adjust R5 to optimize the signal level going into the effect. You may need to keep input levels just a little lower than normal, because the extra high frequencies from the De-Hisser could cause the device to distort at lower levels. Some effects are better suited to the De-Hisser than others; analog delays, tape echo units, reverbs, phase shifters, and flangers seem to work the best, while distortion boxes tend to be more temperamental.

If you're tired of the hiss coming out of your favorite vintage effects box, give this circuit a try. It won't solve all of your noise problems, but it will go a long way toward achieving the ideal of quiet operation.

PARTS LIST

Resistors	(1/4 watt, 5% tolerance recommended)
R1, R2	2.7k (2k7)
R3, R4	10k
R5	10k audio taper pot
R6-R9	27k
R10	100k
R11	470k
R12, R13	1M
Capacitors	(15 working volts minimum)
C1	100pF ceramic disc
C2, C3	3900pF (3n9) polystyrene or mylar

| C4 | 0.05µF (50nF) ceramic disc |
| C5-C8 | 10µF electrolytic |

Other parts

IC1, IC2	NE5532 or equivalent (see text)
J1-J4	Mono, open circuit, ¼" phone jacks
Misc.	IC socket, knob, circuit board, case, solder, etc.

✳ PROJECT 26
ADDING PRESETS TO VINTAGE EFFECTS

Although vintage effects have unique sound qualities, they lack some of the features—such as the ability to select presets—that we've become accustomed to in today's gear. Fortunately, there are some ways to add a limited degree of presettability to effects that were invented before the days of the microprocessor.

The concept behind a preset is simple: think of a car radio, where you can select a favorite station by simply pressing a button that's preset to that station. Presets for musical gear are particularly important when playing live, since you don't want to spend too much time turning a dial back and forth to hit the "sweet" spot. The benefit of not having to think as much about your equipment is that you can think more about your music; you don't want to get so involved turning dials that you lose your musical train of thought. So, here are some techniques that can help bring vintage effects into the preset era.

ABOUT DIFFERENT POTENTIOMETER CONFIGURATIONS

The potentiometers (controls) in most vintage effects are wired in one of two ways (Fig. 8-7).

The basic idea is to decide which control (potentiometer) you want to make presettable, replace it with two or more potentiometers, and add a switch to select among the various pots. By adjusting the pots for your favorite settings, you can switch to those sounds in the time it takes to flick the switch.

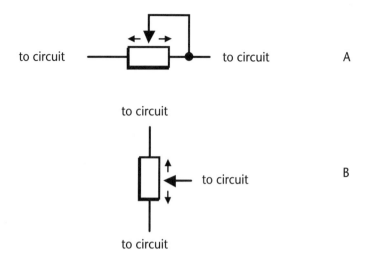

to circuit   to circuit   A

to circuit

to circuit   B

to circuit

TECHNIQUES
FOR ADDING PRESETS

To install a second preset position to Fig. 8-1A, you'd add
another potentiometer of the same value, and an SPDT switch to
select between the two pots (Fig. 8-8). Even better, see if you
can replace the panel potentiometer with one that has a push-
pull switch to do the preset selection. The second control could
be an internally-mounted trimpot set to your favorite setting,
while the original control could remain on the front panel for
choosing different settings. (Trimpots are little potentiometers
that aren't designed for continuous use, but for set-and-forget
applications—you set them to the position you want and leave
them that way, which is perfect for this type of circuit.)

panel control

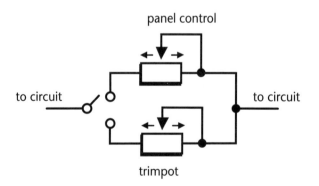

to circuit   to circuit

trimpot

We can take this one step further and use a rotary switch to
select among the front panel control and several internally
mounted trimpots (Fig. 8-9).

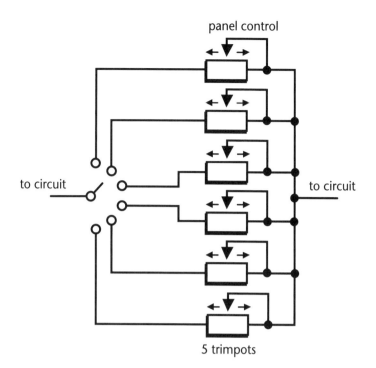

panel control

to circuit

to circuit

5 trimpots

Fig. 8-9
A rotary switch can choose between multiple preset positions. This circuit shows one panel pot and five trimpots, and requires a SP6T (single pole, six throw) switch.

When the potentiometer is hooked up as a three-terminal device (Fig. 8-7B), matters get a bit more complicated. It now becomes necessary to switch between two leads instead of just one, so use a switching circuit like the one in Fig. 8-10.

Here we're using a DPDT (double-pole, double-throw) switch. This can switch two different wires to either of two different positions. For switching more than two potentiometers, you'd need a two-pole, multi-position switch. For example, if you wanted five additional preset positions, you'd need a switch with two poles and six positions (a DP6T switch). The rest of the pots would be wired up similarly to Fig. 8-10.

to circuit

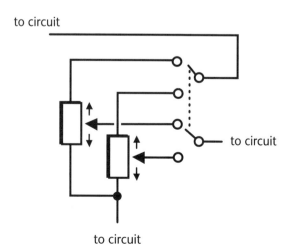

to circuit

to circuit

Fig. 8-10
Using a DPDT switch to select between two preset potentiometers.

Although these applications may seem somewhat simplistic, nothing beats clicking a switch when you need to access a particular control setting as rapidly as possible—it's much faster than turning a dial. What's more, by having one variable control in addition to the presets, you can still obtain any setting you want.

DO-IT-YOURSELF PROJECTS FOR GUITARISTS

Testers

✳ PROJECT **27**
GO/NO GO
GUITAR CORD TESTER

Is it a bad guitar cord that's messing with your sound? With this little box—small enough to throw in your guitar case—you'll know in seconds.

If you want a deluxe cord tester, see the Tri-Test Cord Checker (Project #30). But if all you want is a simple, go/no go indicator, this is the project for you. It tests standard, mono guitar cables for both continuity and shorts.

ABOUT THE CIRCUIT

Fig. 9-1 shows the schematic. Plug the cord to be tested into J1 and J2. When you press the "test" button, current flows from the battery through R1 and the cable's hot lead, then through D1, then back to the battery through the ground lead. If there is continuity, the LED will light. If there is a short, the cable will put a short across the LED so that it can't light. Therefore, as long as the LED lights, you know the cable is good (providing there's not a sneaky intermittent problem—but the Tri-Test was designed to catch those).

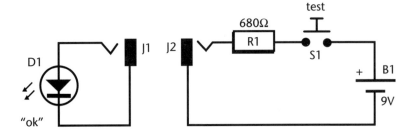

For something even simpler, you can dispense with S1. Just remember to unplug the cable after testing it, or the battery will run down (unless the cable has an open circuit).

By the way, it probably makes the most sense to use a green LED for D1 since people associate green with "go."

PARTS LIST

R1	680Ω resistor
D1	Green LED
J1, J2	Mono, open circuit, ¼" phone jack
S1	SPST pushbutton (see text)
B1	9V battery
Misc.	Battery connector, case, wire, solder, etc.

✴ PROJECT 28
TESTING IMPEDANCE

Proper impedance matching is one of the best-kept secrets for getting a great guitar sound. Here's how to find out conclusively if your system is properly matched to your guitar.

Is your guitar sounding run down? Tired? Dull and anemic? It may not have the flu, but be feeding the wrong kind of input. A guitar pickup puts out relatively weak signals, and the input it feeds (amp or signal processor) can either coddle those signals or stomp on them. It all relates to the unit's *input impedance,* so this project describes a simple tester for determining whether your guitar is driving a signal coddler or a signal stomper.

You might think that testing input impedance is pretty esoteric and that you need an expensive impedance tester, or at least have to fill out one of those matchbooks that says "Learn

Electronics at Home in Your Spare Time." But in this case, testing for impedance is pretty simple. You'll need a standard issue analog or digital volt-ohmmeter (also called multimeter), as sold by Radio Shack and other electronics stores. A good digital model costs around $30-$40. This is one piece of test equipment no guitarist should be without anyway, because you can use it to do anything from test pickups to make sure that the AC line is properly grounded. You'll also need a steady test tone generator, which can be anything from an FM tuner emitting interstation hiss, to a synthesizer set for a constant tone, to a commercial test tone oscillator.

WHAT IS IMPEDANCE?

If theory scares you, skip ahead to the next subhead. Stay tuned if you can, though, since impedance is an important part of audio electronics.

An amp or effect's input impedance provides the same electrical result as draping a resistance from the input to ground, thus shunting some of your signal to ground. The lower this resistance to ground, the more the signal gets shunted and the greater the loss.

The guitar's output impedance, which is equivalent to putting a resistance in series with your guitar and the amp input, works in conjunction with the input impedance to impede the signal. If you draw an equivalent circuit for these two resistances, it looks suspiciously like the schematic for a volume control (Fig. 9-2).

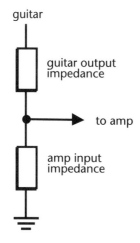

guitar

guitar output impedance

to amp

amp input impedance

Fig. 9-2
Equivalent circuit for a guitar's output impedance and amplifier input impedance.

If the guitar's output impedance is low and the amp input impedance is high, there is little loss. Conversely, a high guitar output impedance and low amp input impedance creates a lot of loss.

The reason why a low input impedance "dulls" the sound is because a pickup's output impedance increases with frequency. Thus, low frequency signals may not be attenuated that much, but high frequencies could get clobbered.

One way to prevent impedance problems is to use a buffer board or on-board preamp (both of which turn the guitar output into a low impedance output for all frequencies). Yet many devices *are* properly designed to handle guitar, so adding more circuitry would be redundant. The trick is separating the guitar-friendly effects from the guitar-hostile ones, especially with signal processors that were primarily designed for studio applications—even though there may be enough gain to kick the meters into the red, that doesn't necessarily mean that the input impedance is sufficient to preserve your tone. Hence, the following test rig.

IMPEDANCE TESTING

Fig. 9-3
Test jig for measuring the input impedance of an amp or signal processor.

This test takes advantage of the fact that impedance and resistance are, at least in this application, roughly equivalent. So, if we can determine the input resistance to ground, we're covered. (Just clipping an ohmmeter across a dummy plug inserted in the input jack isn't good enough; the input will usually be capacitor-coupled, making it impossible to measure resistance without taking the device's cover off.)

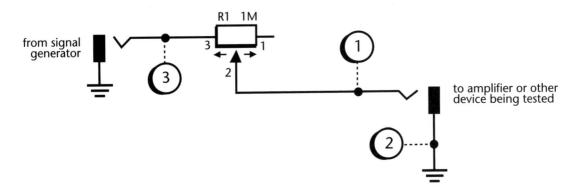

Wire up the test jig in Fig. 9-3, which consists of a 1 Meg linear taper pot and two ¼" phone jacks. Plug in the signal generator and amplifier (or other device being tested), then perform the following steps. Any master volume controls should be all the way down.

1   Set the multimeter to the 10V AC range so it can measure audio signals. You may later need to switch to a more sensitive range (*e.g.,* 2.5V or so) if the test oscillator signal isn't strong enough for the meter to give a reliable reading.

2   Set R1 to zero ohms (no resistance).

3   Measure the signal generator level by clipping the multimeter leads to test points 1 and 2. The polarity doesn't matter since we're measuring AC signals. Aim for a signal generator level between 1 and 2 volts AC.

4   Rotate R1 until the meter reads exactly 50% of what it did in step 3.

5   Be very careful not to disturb R1's setting as you unplug the signal generator and amplifier input from the test jig.

6   Set the multimeter to measure ohms, then clip the leads to test points 1 and 3.

7   Measure R1's resistance. This will essentially equal the input impedance of the device being tested.

INTERPRETING THE RESULTS

If the impedance is under 100k, I'd *strongly* recommend adding a preamp or buffer board between your guitar and amp or effect to eliminate dulling and signal loss. The range of 100k to 200k is acceptable, although you may hear some high frequency loss. An input impedance over 200k means the designer either knew what guitarists really need, or got lucky. Note, however, that more is not always better. Input impedances above approximately 500k are sometimes prone to picking up radio frequency interference and noise, without offering much of a sonic advantage.

So there you have it: amaze your friends, impress your main squeeze, and strike fear into the forces of evil with your new-found knowledge. A guitar that feeds the right input impedance comes alive, with a crispness, presence, and fidelity that's a joy to hear. Happy testing—and picking.

✳ PROJECT 29
LED LEVEL METER

They say a picture is worth a thousand words, so here's a way to get a picture of your guitar's level—and improve your playing "touch" in the process.

This project uses National Semiconductor's NSM3916 LED VU meter board module to display your guitar's signal level. The NSM3916 includes a linear array of 10 rectangular LEDs along with an associated meter driver IC; we need to add only a few more parts (and power supply) to make a complete level meter. To save energy, we'll be running it in the dot mode, where only one LED is lit at a time.

Most LED VU meters are packaged so that the line of LEDs runs in an up and down direction, with the lower LEDs illuminating in the presence of lower level signals, and the upper LEDs lighting when stronger signals occur. The visual effect of watching these LEDs dance up and down in response to level changes is really entrancing, but there are several practical uses for this gizmo. For example, you can graphically see the wide dynamic range of a guitar signal—playing chords lights the very highest LEDs, while single note runs may only light up the two or three lowest LEDs.

This meter also clearly demonstrates the effects of compression and fuzz, and how they limit a signal's dynamic range; you can also "see" echoes coming out of an echo unit, with each echo diminishing somewhat in strength. Perhaps best of all, monitoring your signal with an LED meter allows you to become conscious of your "touch."

HOW IT WORKS

Referring to Fig. 9-4, IC1 buffers the input signal and amplifies it a bit; IC2 is an interesting circuit called a *DC restorer* that translates

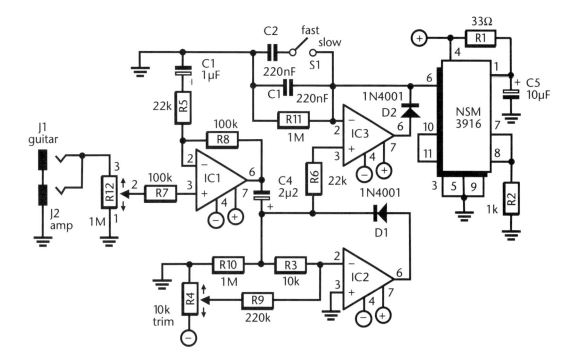

the input into a peak-to-peak voltage. This output then feeds IC3, a peak detector, which converts the peak-to-peak AC audio signal into the smooth DC signal by the NSM3916's detector.

Fig. 9-4
LED level meter
schematic.

The simplest setup is to plug your guitar into J1 and then run a cord from J2 to your amp. However, since this circuit presents very little loading, you can actually tap off just about any point in the signal chain—such as just before the power amp, from an effect output, and so on.

CONSTRUCTION

This circuit is relatively non-critical as long as you keep your ground leads short and direct. The op amps can be 741 types (noise doesn't matter for this application), half of a dual op amp such as an NE5532, or bifet types such as the TL071 or LF356.

USING THE LED METER

This circuit will work fine with virtually any bipolar 9V supply, including Project #12, AC Power Supply. Battery operation is not recommended, as the circuit draws about 25 mA from the +9V supply, and around 5 mA from the -9V supply. Remember that the points marked (+) connect to the positive power supply, and (-) to the negative power supply.

The NSM3916 is designed so that with no input voltage, no LED is on. However, I prefer to have the bottom (or lowest level) LED, located nearest to the module's pin 1, on at all times since this way you know that the meter is operational. Trimpot R4 allows you to turn the bottom LED on if desired. With R12 all the way down (center wiper at ground), adjust R4 so that the bottom LED is either on or off, depending on your preference.

R12 is a sensitivity control. If you consistently hit the top LED, even with fairly low level signals, turn down this control.

S1 determines the meter response speed. In the fast position, the LEDs respond with a fast attack/moderate decay action. In the slow position, the decay becomes longer so that peak readings are held a little bit longer as well.

This is a fun circuit to play with, but it can also be extremely educational...try one out and you'll see what I mean.

PARTS LIST

Resistors   (1/4 watt, 5% tolerance preferred over 10%)

R1	33Ω
R2	1k
R3	10k
R4	10k trimpot
R5, R6	22k
R7, R8	100k
R9	220k
R10, R11	1M
R12	1M potentiometer

Capacitors (10 or more working volts)

C1, C2	0.22µF (220nF), mylar preferred over disc
C3	1µF, electrolytic or tantalum
C4	2.2µF (2µ2), electrolytic or tantalum
C5	5 to 50µF, electrolytic or tantalum

Semiconductors

D1, D2	1N4001 or equivalent diode
IC1-IC3	741 or equivalent type op amp (see text)
NSM3916	National Semiconductor LED VU meter module

Other parts

J1, J2	Mono, open circuit, ¼" phone jack

PARTS LIST *(continued)*

S1   SPST switch

Misc.   Circuit board, knob, solder, sockets, wire, case, power

            supply, etc.

✳ PROJECT 30
"TRI-TEST" CORD CHECKER

A cord checker…yawn. Well, before you skip the page, note that this
one is real different from the simple models that test for only the
two most common cord problems.

The Tri-Test cord checker checks for:

- Continuity (whether the hot and shield wires connecting the
  two plugs are good)

- Internal shorts (whether the hot and ground wires short
  together rather than being properly insulated)

- Intermittents (which is what makes this cord tester special)

Intermittents, which generally produce a "crackly" sound,
occur when a cord has not yet failed but has deteriorated to the
point where interruptions in continuity (or problems with
shorts) occur for very brief periods of time—say, a few millisec-
onds. Although you can hear the crackling noises caused by
intermittents, simple cord testers which use an LED or meter as
an indicator will usually not let you "see" these crackles. Intermittents can be so short that your eye's persistence of vision
will not allow you to see this extremely rapid light change. As
someone who had gotten fed up with crackly patch cords, I
came up with the Tri-Test cord checker as one way to catch
deteriorating patch cords before they worked their way into a
live or studio setup.

HOW IT WORKS

Referring to Fig. 9-5, with DPDT switch S1 in the C (continuity)
position and a cord plugged into J1 and J2, the battery sends a

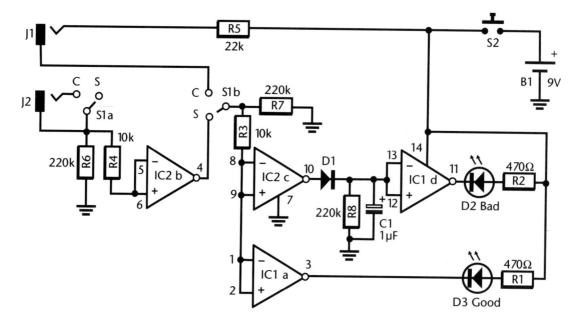

positive voltage (through R5) to the hot conductor of the cable under test. The hot conductor carries this voltage to J2. Since S1a (half of DPDT switch S1) connects the hot to the ground at J2, the voltage then flows back through the ground conductor until it hits J1's ground connection. If there is continuity throughout this path, then IC1a and IC1c (which are configured as inverters) see a positive voltage at their inputs. This condition allows IC1a's output to sink current, thus lighting the "good" LED, but also prevents IC1d's output from sinking current so the "bad" LED can't light.

Now, suppose there's a brief interruption in continuity. The "good" LED will flash off, although as noted earlier, this will probably happen too rapidly for you to see. More importantly, the output of IC1c will go positive for the length of the interruption. This sends a positive voltage to C1 via D1, which lets IC1d sink current and thus turn on the "bad" LED. However, even after the interruption stops, C1 retains its charge for a while; this allows the "bad" LED to stay on for about half a second, thus showing that an interruption has occurred and signaling an intermittent condition. (If you want the LED to stay on longer, increase R8's value—up to 1 Meg or so.)

With S1 in the S (short) position, any short will cause a positive voltage to flow from the battery to IC1b's input. This forces IC1a's output positive, thus preventing D3 from lighting, and also forces IC1c's output positive, thus allowing IC1d's output to sink current and turn on the "bad" LED. If the short occurs for only a short (sorry about the pun) period of time, C1 will again stretch the time the "bad" LED is on to make it easier to note the problem.

CONSTRUCTION TIPS

Build the tester in a plastic case (preferred), or if you use a metal (conductive) case, use insulated jacks. Radio Shack sells suitable plastic enclosures. Also, note that IC1 is a CMOS part, so handle it carefully—avoid excessive handling, and keep the chip in its protective conductive foam until you are ready to insert the chip into its socket. Another caution is to observe polarity on the capacitor, diode, and LEDs. As usual, use rosin core (*not* acid core) solder, and be careful not to apply too much heat to any of the parts.

USING THE TRI-TEST

Plug the cord to be tested into the two jacks, then close S2 (I prefer a pushbutton switch for this function). Check the cord in both positions of S1. If the "bad" light comes on, the cord is bad (tip: cut the cord in half and make up a new, shorter cord using the half that tests out okay). If the "good" light comes on, you know there is continuity and no internal shorting. Now jiggle the cord a bit to check for intermittents. If the "bad" light comes on at any point during the jiggling process, the cord has an intermittent condition. Check for intermittents in both positions of S1.

A cord tester may not be the most glamorous device in the world—but if this little gizmo saves you from the embarrassment of going on stage with a crackly cord, you'll definitely appreciate its talents.

PARTS LIST

Resistors (1/4 watt, 5% or 10%)

R1, R2   470Ω

R3, R4   10k

PARTS LIST *(continued)*

R5	22k
R6-R8	220k

Capacitor   (10 or more working volts)

C1	1μF (electrolytic or tantalum)

Semiconductors

D1	1N914 or 1N4001 diode
D2, D3	LEDs
IC1	CD4001 quad NOR gate (configured as four inverters)

Other parts

J1, J2	Mono, open circuit, ¼″ phone jacks (see text)
S1	DPDT switch
S2	SPST switch (see text)
Misc.	Plastic enclosure, socket, battery connector, circuit board, etc.

10

Advanced Projects

✳ PROJECT 31
DESIGN AN ON-BOARD GUITAR PREAMP

If you want an on-board preamp that fits your exact needs, why not design your own? It's not all that difficult, and you can learn a lot in the process.

This project is for those who want to know what makes guitar electronics tick and have an interest in engineering, math, and circuit design. We'll not only present schematics, but lead you through the design process so that you can make modifications to suit your specific requirements. As you go along, you'll also learn a lot about musical electronics.

ABOUT ON-BOARD ELECTRONICS AND PREAMPS

In the quest for the ultimate electric guitar, some designers have opted for adding active, on-board electronic circuitry to improve the instrument's overall performance. Benefits of on-board electronics include greater output strength, less susceptibility to loading by guitar cords and subsequent amps or signal processors, and improvement of the pickup's tonal qualities. Disadvantages include the need for battery power, the possibility of adding noise or distortion to the guitar signal, and the fact that a guitar has to be modified in some way to make room for the extra circuitry and battery(s).

Although you could add a preamp in the signal path between the guitar and guitar amplifier to minimize loading and other problems, you still need a cord between the guitar output and preamp input. Since the preamp should have a relatively high input impedance, the input cord can act like an antenna for unwanted signals.

Mounting a preamp *inside* the guitar minimizes the length of the connecting wire between the pickup outputs and preamp input. Additionally, the preamp's output impedance is very low; this low impedance output is ideal for driving long cords, just about any type of amplifier, and can often overcome the problems associated with feeding multiple effects systems.

Another possible advantage is that preamps boost volume to a greater or lesser degree, so it's possible for the preamplified guitar signal to overload the guitar amp it feeds. This overloading can produce a smooth kind of distortion (particularly with tube amps) that many professional guitarists use to give a more sustained sound.

TYPICAL CONTROLS AND OPTIONS

The most important characteristic of an on-board preamp is the amount of gain. With too much gain, the guitar pickup can overload the preamp, thus producing a distorted sound that cannot be "cleaned up" when you want a clean sound. Preamps are more likely to be overloaded when fed by high output (hot rod) pickups.

With too little gain, the preamp may not give the desired amount of boost. However, too little gain is almost always preferable to too much gain.

Because of the importance of choosing the proper amount of gain, preamps should include some kind of gain altering control or trimpot. Some preamps have a fixed amount of gain; while there's nothing wrong with this, it is important to know the exact amount of gain so you can match the preamp to a specific guitar's pickups.

If the preamp uses a single battery, and the guitar feeding it has hot rod pickups, then you really can't have much more than about 6 dB or so of gain without running the risk of distortion. Weaker pickups can be amplified by about 10 dB before overloading occurs. With dual battery preamps, 10 dB of gain will still give a clean sound with hot rod pickups, and gain can be as high as 15 dB when the preamp is used with stock pickups.

As to why it is important to have a clean preamp sound if you plan to use the preamp principally for distortion effects, the preamp will distort in a different way from an overloaded guitar amp. I think that most guitarists prefer the sound of an over-loaded tube guitar amp over the sound of the semiconductor distortion associated with on-board preamps, and if the two types of distortion are mixed, the overall effect may not be as pure-sounding as the effect derived by simply overloading the amp.

DISADVANTAGES OF ON-BOARD ELECTRONICS

The main problem with on-board electronics is that they need power. While it is possible to use phantom powering (where power connects to the preamp through the same wire that carries the audio), or use a multi-conductor cable to carry audio and power, it is usually more convenient to put a battery inside the guitar. However, unless the on-board device draws very little power, it's a real bother to change batteries regularly. And if the battery goes dead in the middle of a performance, you could have a disaster on your hands (although we'll talk about ways to minimize this kind of problem).

Any electronic circuit generates noise; an on-board preamp or tone control circuit is no exception. While this may not bother guitarists who simply plug their axes into an amp, feeding a high gain device such as a compressor or fuzz may emphasize any noise generated by the guitar electronics. As a result, low-noise operation is (at least to my ears!) the most important aspect of any type of on-board electronics.

Although purists may object to putting active electronics inside a guitar—and I can certainly understand that sentiment—the fact remains that for a reasonably small investment in time and money, an on-board preamp can make a huge difference in sound quality and reduce variability as you use different amps and cables.

DESIGNING AN ON-BOARD PREAMP

Fortunately, on-board preamps are not complex to build, which makes them ideal candidates for do-it-yourself projects.

The main reason to consider building your own preamp is that no one preamp design can be all things to all guitarists. One player might use hot rod pickups and want a clean sound, another might want a dirty sound, and a third might want to change a guitar's tonal characteristics (such as Strat owners who want more of a Les Paul sound). A simple preamp cannot satisfy all these users, and making the preamp complex enough to cover all possibilities would probably create too many controls to fit in the average guitar. The answer is to custom design your own preamp.

Designing a preamp may sound difficult, but it isn't. First we'll discuss the subject from the engineer's point of view for those who want some background on these circuits, then we'll approach the actual design of the preamp in more of a "cookbook" style, where we give a schematic and you merely plug some numbers into a few simple equations to tailor the preamp response to your application.

BIPOLAR TRANSISTOR, FET, OR IC PREAMP?

The first question to consider is what type of semiconductor device is best for amplifying the guitar's signal. While transistor and FET preamps can give excellent results, IC op amps are exceptionally easy to use from a design standpoint and are less "touchy."

INVERTING OR
NON-INVERTING PREAMP?

Semiconductor data books show three basic types of op amp preamp: *inverting, non-inverting,* and *differential.* Each has unique disadvantages and advantages. The differential type is the most complicated of the three, and doesn't really offer any significant advantages in our application. So, let's look at the standard inverting and non-inverting amplifier structures (Fig. 10-1).

Fig. 10-1
Inverting and non-inverting preamp structures.

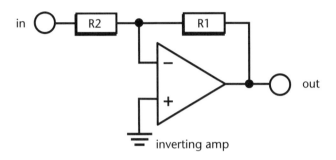

inverting amp

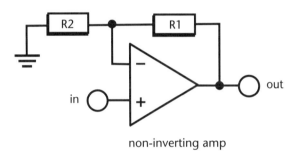

non-inverting amp

If you wonder how these names came about, the output of an inverting amp is 180 degrees out of phase with respect to the input signal; the output of a non-inverting amp is in phase compared to the input. This is mentioned for reference only, since the output phase doesn't matter in this type of circuit.

An inverting preamp's gain equals R1/R2, and the input signal flows through input resistor R2. Ideally, a preamp should have a relatively high impedance (at least 100kΩ) to avoid loading down pickups, so this input resistor must be at least 100kΩ. However, using a high value input resistor for R2 means that R1 must be extremely high to get a reasonable amount of preamp gain *(e.g.,* for a gain of 10 and R2 = 100k, R1 would have to be 1M).

Unfortunately, these high resistances contribute a fair amount of noise to the preamp, since op amps give the least amount of noise when their (-) and (+) terminals see a low DC resistance to ground. Values between 1k and 10k are optimum for most popular op amps. (Incidentally, bifet op amps offer better noise performance with high input resistances than their bipolar cousins, but with either type of op amp low input resistances are preferable for a number of reasons.) Although the (+) input of the inverting amp in Fig. 10-1 sees a low resistance to ground, the (-) input does not since R1 and R2 need to be high value resistors in order to create gain. So much for the inverting amp.

With non-inverting amps, the gain equals (R1 + R2)/R2. This brings up one disadvantage of the non-inverting amp: you cannot obtain a gain of less than 1 *(i.e., you cannot use a non-inverting amp to attenuate, only to amplify)*. However, since we want gain, not attenuation, this limitation doesn't affect us.

The non-inverting amp's biggest advantage is that you can feed the input signal directly into the (+) input, which unlike the op amp's (-) input, presents a very high input impedance (millions of ohms). Also, the gain setting resistors (R1 and R2) are independent of the signal input. So, we can use low value resistors here and satisfy our requirement for a low resistance DC path from the (-) input to ground.

As an added bonus, you can connect the hot lead of a pickup (or combination of pickups) directly to the (+) input with no intervening capacitors or resistors, which provides several important benefits:

- The pickup itself represents a DC resistance of around a few thousand ohms. So, the (+) input sees a low resistance path to ground through the pickup itself, which is important for minimum noise.

- The pickup's output signal sees the very high input impedance provided by the (+) input, which means minimal loading of the pickups and better sound.

ONE OR TWO BATTERIES?

The maximum amount of undistorted gain a preamp can deliver depends on the power supply. A single 9V battery can deliver an output signal that is at least 7V peak-to-peak (p-p for short; this is the measurement from the most positive peak of an audio waveform to the most negative peak, as shown in Fig. 10-2).

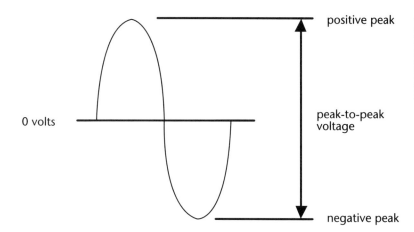

positive peak

0 volts

peak-to-peak voltage

negative peak

Fig. 10-2 Measuring a waveform's peak-to-peak voltage.

This is more than enough to drive most tape recorders, studio mixing consoles, and hi-fi type power amps. Where a very large output signal is required in order to, say, overdrive an amp, two batteries will give you at least 14V peak-to-peak of output signal. There are several reasons why using two batteries can be advantageous:

- Even if your average preamp output signal is around 7V p-p, chances are your guitar will produce big transients from time to time that exceed this average level when you first pluck the string. Two batteries give enough headroom to accommodate these peaks.

- Since most studio equipment is designed with a fair amount of headroom, if your main reason for adding a preamp is to drive studio-type equipment, then it's worth having the two batteries.

- You don't have to change two batteries as often as one since they share the total current consumption.

- Most op amps are designed to accept bipolar power supplies (*i.e.,* positive and negative voltages with respect to ground), which two batteries can provide. Using a single battery requires additional parts to fool the op amp into thinking that it is being fed from a bipolar supply.

Unfortunately, you may not be able to fit two batteries into some guitars, in which case you will be forced to use a single battery. We'll show how to use single, as well as dual, battery supplies for the preamp so that you'll be covered no matter what.

Now that we've covered the technology, let's look into the details of preamp design, and how to specify parts that customize the preamp to your specific needs. Fig. 10-3 shows our point of departure—a basic non-inverting preamp.

Fig. 10-3
Basic preamp
design.

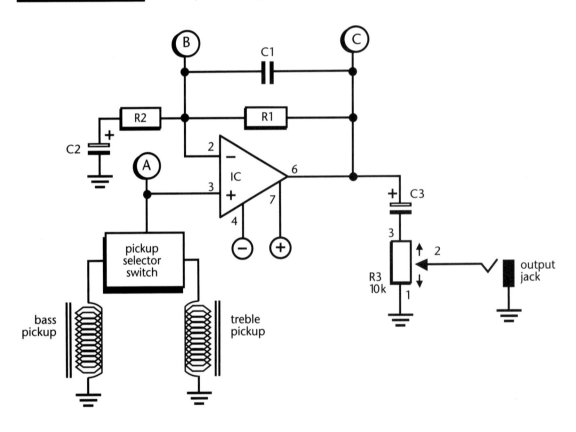

SETTING GAIN

We need two pieces of data to determine the optimum amount of gain: how many volts peak-to-peak your pickup generates on peaks, and how many batteries you'll be using.

Assume you're using one battery, which provides headroom of at least 7V p-p. If your pickup puts out 7V p-p as is, then it's already butting up against the available headroom, so we had better not include any gain at all. In this case, you're better off building a non-amplifying Buffer Board (Project #7).

Chances are, though, that your pickup will produce less voltage. If it puts out 3.5V p-p, then you can give this signal a gain of two before exceeding the 7V p-p headroom limit; 1.5V p-p from your pickup means that a gain of four would still be "safe." If you don't know your pickup's signal level, you can assume that a preamp with a gain of two will handle all but the hottest pickups, and that a gain of three will be safe for stock single coil types. If you're using two batteries, you can double the amount of gain without exceeding the preamp's headroom.

Remember that the formula for gain is (R1 + R2)/R2; let's choose R2 as 10k, since that represents a good DC resistance value to ground. Therefore, for a gain of two R1 should be 10k, since (10k + 10k)/10k = 2. For a gain of 6, R1 should be 50k (47k is close enough), since (50k + 10k)/10k = 6. You can figure out other gain values yourself.

SPECIFYING LOW FREQUENCY ROLLOFF

There's little point in having the preamp amplify frequencies outside the range of your guitar, so C2 attenuates extremely low frequencies. The following formula gives the frequency at which the response will be down by 3 dB:

Frequency (Hz) = 1/(6.28 X R2 X C2)

…where R2 is in megohms and C2 is in µF. To solve for C2, we do a little algebra and transform the formula into:

C2 = 1/(6.28 X R2 X Freq)

A good rolloff frequency is 40 Hz, a little over a full octave below the lowest note on a guitar. Since we know R2 = 10k = 0.01 Meg, we can substitute these numbers in our equation:

C2 = 1/(6.28 X 0.01 X 40)

With an assist from a trusty calculator, we end up with C2 = 0.39µF. However, 0.39µF is not a standard value part; so, we can either wire two 0.22µF capacitors in parallel for a value of 0.44µF, or use a 1µF capacitor which will instead give a rolloff of 15 Hz. A 0.22µF capacitor would give a rolloff frequency of 72 Hz—probably low enough for our purposes. No matter which of these options you choose, the sonic difference will be negligible.

C3 can also roll off low frequencies; the degree depends on the input impedance of the next stage. Since we don't want the response to change too much with different loads, we'll use 1µF for C3. This will deliver consistent results, even when driving a relatively low impedance input. Note that if this preamp is for bass, C2 should be approximately 1µF and C3 should be 2 to 5µF.

SPECIFYING HIGH FREQUENCY ROLLOFF

C1 rolls off the high frequencies as a preventive measure against unwanted oscillation. The formula for figuring out the value of this capacitor is:

$$C1 = 1/(6.28 \times R1 \times Freq)$$

Again, C1 is in µF, R1 in megohms, and Freq is in Hz. Assuming a rolloff frequency of 30 kHz and R1 = 10k, we end up with:

$$C1 = 1/(6.28 \times .01 \times 30,000), \text{ or } C1 = 0.0005µF = 500pF$$

500pF is a non-standard value, but 470pF is close enough. Had R1 been equal to 22k, then C1 would need to be 240pF (220pF is the nearest standard value).

TONE CONTROL OPTIONS

There are several ways to alter the preamp's tone. One method is to simply strap another capacitor in parallel with C1 to roll off the high frequencies even more, and connect a switch in parallel with this capacitor to cut it in or out (see Fig. 10-4). We use the same formula given above; for example, if you want the response to start dropping off at 3 kHz and R1 = 10k, then

$$C4 = 1/(6.28 \times 0.01 \times 3,000), \text{ or } 0.005µF (5nF).$$

C tone

Fig. 10-4
Tone control
switch.

Fig. 10-5 shows other ways to control tone. In 5A, we've
hooked a standard tone control circuit across the pickups. The
pot should be around 250k to 500k, while the capacitor will vary
depending upon the type of pickups that you use. Start with
0.022μF (22nF) and experiment from there. More capacitance
will cut off more highs, while less capacitance will leave more
highs intact. Fig. 10-5B replaces the pot with a switch; again,
choose the capacitor by experimentation. Fig. 10-5C shows how
to use an SPDT switch to choose between two different tone
control capacitors. This could be a center-off switch if you
wanted a "no capacitor" position.

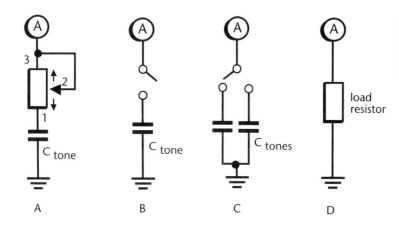

A B C D

Fig. 10-5
Various tone control
options.

Fig. 10-5D shows a more devious way to cut high frequencies by loading down a pickup. Normally this is undesirable, but
if you're a Strat owner looking for a Les Paul sound, loading
down the pickup will give a duller sound that might be just what
you want. Try putting a 10k resistor from point A to ground and
see if that gives the effect you want. If the effect is too drastic,
then move up to 22k. This resistor will also cut down on the
pickup output, so you may need to increase the preamp gain to
compensate.

BATTERIES

Fig. 10-6A shows how to hook up two batteries. Note that you
need a DPDT or DPST switch to turn these on and off. Fig. 10-6B

shows how to hook up a single battery. In this case, you need additional parts but an advantage is that you can get by with a less expensive SPST on-off switch. Some jacks include a separate switch function that's activated by plugging in a plug, which lets you turn on the preamp simply by patching into the guitar's output jack.

Fig. 10-6
Two ways to provide power to an on-board preamp.

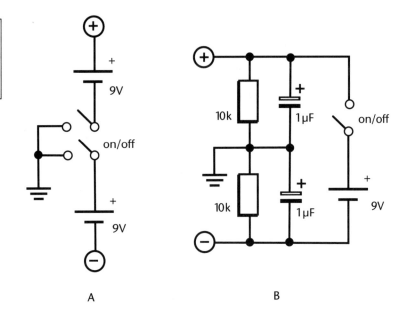

A   B

CHOOSING THE OP AMP

Use a socket for the op amp so you can experiment with different chips. As we all know, this is an imperfect world and op amps are no exception—it's difficult to find a part that is affordable, quiet, draws little current, and can drive heavy loads. Generally you need to make a tradeoff somewhere, and the most common is lower noise for increased current consumption.

One popular op amp choice is the LF351, a bifet op amp that offers quiet operation and draws only 1.8 mA, thereby ensuring long battery life. The LF356 is even quieter, but draws a little over 3 mA. Other good choices are the TL071 (optimized for low noise) and TL081 (not as quiet, but easier to find).

WIRING TIME

When you wire up the preamp, keep the inputs and outputs physically separate to avoid feedback. Also, mount R1 and C1 as close to the IC as possible.

Since the preamp will be going in a small space, make sure that no exposed metal parts can short out to anything else inside the guitar's cavity.

WHERE TO CONNECT THE PREAMP IN THE SIGNAL PATH

For the best performance from an on-board preamp, it has to be installed correctly in the guitar's signal path. Fig. 10-7 shows a typical guitar wiring scheme for a double pickup guitar. The pickup switch selects one or both pickups; then comes the tone control, volume control, and output jack.

Fig. 10-7
Standard passive guitar wiring.

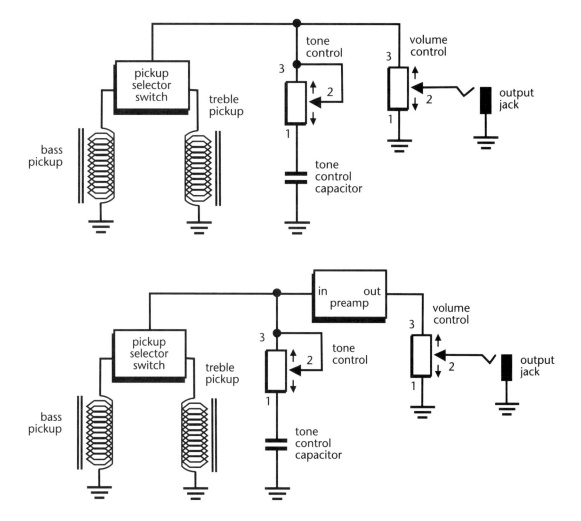

Fig. 10-8
One option for inserting the preamp in the guitar's signal path.

If you are using low output pickups, and your preamp offers moderate gain (say, up to 10 dB or so), then the best place to put the preamp is between the tone control and volume control (Fig. 10-8). This way, if the preamp has a high impedance input, the tone control will still be effective; also, as you turn down the output control, you'll simultaneously turn down any noise generated by the preamp.

For even better performance, replace the guitar's standard 250kΩ to 500kΩ volume control with a 10kΩ to 50kΩ control. This insures that cable capacitance will have less of an effect as you turn down the control. A lower value pot also provides a better match for driving subsequent effects or amp inputs.

However, since the pickups feed directly into the preamp with this approach, you can run into overload problems if you use high output pickups or if the preamp has lots of gain. Fig. 10-9 shows how to solve this problem by mounting the preamp between the output control and output jack. In this case, you must use the same value volume control as the guitar's stock control.

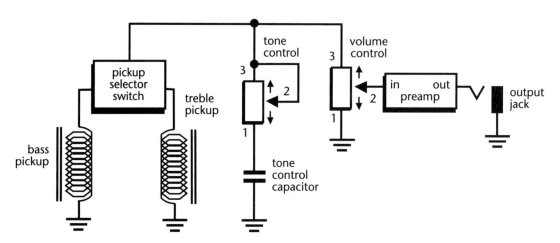

By placing the volume control in front of the preamp, you can regulate the amount of signal feeding the preamp. There's a tradeoff, though. Because the preamp output always feeds the output jack, any preamp noise will always travel through to the amp, so turning down the output control will not turn down the preamp noise at the same time.

ADDING PREAMP BYPASS SWITCHES

Since an on-board preamp could fail (usually because of a bad battery, but occasionally from a bad part), you'll probably feel a

lot more secure with a bypass switch that can cut the preamp
out of circuit and return the guitar to its stock wiring. Fig. 10-10
shows how to add a preamp bypass switch to the setup shown
in Fig. 10-8. Note that you must use the same value output control as the one originally supplied with the guitar in order for
everything to work out right; you can't use the 10kΩ to 50kΩ
pot recommended earlier, since this would load down the guitar
pickups in the bypassed position. This is not a problem if you
bypass the preamp in Fig. 10-9 in this manner.

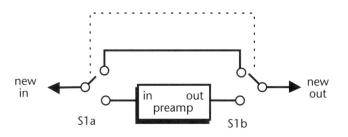

Fig. 10-10
Adding a bypass
switch to cut the
preamp out of the
signal path.

An additional benefit of bypass switches occurs if you use
your preamp principally to create distortion, or to overload an
amp. When the preamp is in circuit, you'll get your distorted
sound. When it's bypassed, the sound will be cleaner.

BATTERY BACKUP CIRCUIT

Since most failures are due to having a battery go dead, the circuit in Fig. 10-11 shows a way around the problem if you're
using a single-battery power supply. The SPDT switch allows
switching over to a backup battery in case the primary battery

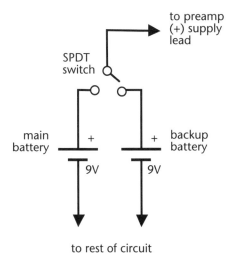

Fig. 10-11
Switching between a
main and backup
battery.

fails. This technique is not recommended for preamps using two batteries.

✳ PROJECT 32
OCTAVE-DOUBLING FUZZ

Why be normal? Here's a distortion box that is anything but normal. It not only distorts your sound, but gives octave-above and ring modulator effects that can range from evocative to downright nasty.

This is one of those occasions where it would be really great if you could hear what this project does, because trying to describe it in print is very difficult. It's somewhat like conventional distortion, but you'll also hear some octave above and pseudo-ring modulation effects, especially with notes higher up on the neck. Let's just leave it at this: if you like distortion and want something different, this device isn't too difficult to build and is definitely something out of the ordinary.

HOW IT WORKS

The Octave-Doubling Fuzz (Fig. 10-12) consists of a buffer stage built around IC1a along with fuzz channel 1 (IC2a), fuzz channel 2 (IC1b), and an output mixer (IC2b) that blends together the two fuzz channels. Fuzz channel 1 is a conventional distortion stage that includes an overdrive control to set the distortion intensity and a switch, S2, to cut this channel in and out of the mixer. Fuzz channel 2 is an unusual kind of fuzz whose doubling properties we'll get into later; it includes a level control that can inject any desired amount of fuzz channel 2's output into the mixer.

TIPS FOR BEST RESULTS

You'll get best results with the bass (neck) guitar pickup, especially if you turn the tone control all the way down (minimum treble). Start experimenting with other pickups and tone settings

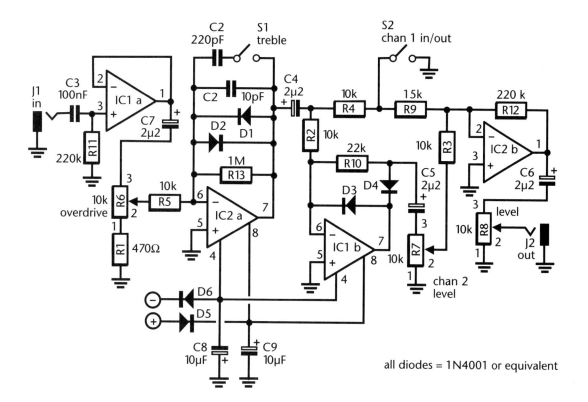

Fig. 10-12

Octave-Doubling

Fuzz schematic.

only after you get a feeling for the unit's overall operation. Closing S1 adds C2 to the circuit and reduces the treble further if desired (for even less treble, increase C2's value).

Another caution concerns output level: this circuit can deliver lots of signal—more than enough to overload the average guitar amp—so keep the output level control fairly low at first, or you might confuse the sound of the fuzz with distortion created by overloading the amp. Once you know what the fuzz can do by itself, then by all means experiment with overloading subsequent stages.

CONSTRUCTION NOTES

The circuit uses NE5532 op amps for lowest noise, but if you're tight for space you could use a quad op amp like the TL074 or TL084. If you're not picky about noise, you can use individual 741 op amps or dual 741-type op amps like the 5558. Just about any internally-compensated op amp will do, but remember, the pinout will probably be different from that indicated on the schematic.

TESTING THE OCTAVE-DOUBLING FUZZ

Check fuzz channel 2. Turn R6 all the way counterclockwise (wiper at R1 end) and close S2 so that fuzz channel 1 shorts to ground instead of feeding the mixer. Next, turn the channel 2 level control (R7) up full; you'll notice that while this does not produce a normal fuzz sound, it does create one which is still quite distorted. Most important of all, though, this fuzz is *dynamically responsive.* With most fuzzes, whether you play a soft note or a loud one, they usually come out at the same level. However with fuzz channel 2, the harder you pick, the louder the note sounds. To create a more distorted sound, turn up R6.

Check fuzz channel 1. Return R6 to full down, and open S2. Then turn R7 full down (wiper closest to ground terminal); you should hear a basically clean sound. Now turn up R6, and you'll get sounds that are very similar to a conventional fuzz. Although fuzz channels 1 and 2 make some pretty neat sounds, we still have further to go.

Combine channels 1 and 2. Leave S2 open, and turn R6 all the way down. Next, turn R7 all the way up, then play some single-note runs around the 12th fret area of your guitar's neck. The overall sound should now include a tone that is an octave higher than the actual note being fingered on your guitar. This effect comes into play around the 7th fret. Lower notes won't sound bad, but you won't get as prominent a harmonic accent effect.

Start turning down R7, and you'll notice that the harmonic emphasis goes away until the control is all the way off, at which point you're left with only the channel 2 sound. Return R7 to full up, and then begin to experiment with the overdrive control; by turning it up, you should get the same type of octave-doubled sound, but with more intensity. The doubling effect works best when the signal levels out of fuzz channel 1 and fuzz channel 2 are *exactly* matched, so experiment with R7 until you get the best overall sound.

An additional byproduct of combining channels 1 and 2 is the series of effects you obtain by playing intervals. For starters, fret a standard D major barre chord at the 10th fret and strum the top three strings. This produces a chime-like, ring modulation sort of sound. Try this at other places on the neck, then try playing fifths, ninths, and octaves; they each acquire different characteristics when mixing fuzz channels 1 and 2 together.

Because fuzz channel 2 has dynamics, you can follow this fuzz with an envelope-controlled effect and get better results than you would with a conventional fuzz. Be sure to try the Octave-Doubling Fuzz with other effects; I think you're going to have a pretty good time adding these new sounds to your musical vocabulary.

PARTS LIST

Resistors (all resistors are 1/4W, 10% except as noted)

R1	470Ω
R2-R5	10k
R6-R8	10k audio taper pot (linear types are acceptable)
R9	15k
R10	22k
R11, R12	220k
R13	1M

Capacitors (rated at 10 or more volts)

C1	10pF disc
C2	220pF disc
C3	0.1μF (100nF) disc or mylar
C4-C7	2.2μF (2μ2) electrolytic or tantalum
C8, C9	10μF electrolytic or tantalum

Semiconductors

D1-D6	1N4001 or equivalent silicon diode
IC1, IC2	NE5532 op amp (see text)

Other parts

S1, S2	SPST toggle switch
J1, J2	Mono, open circuit, ¼" phone jack
Misc.	Sockets, knobs, solder, wire, hardware, case, etc.

* PROJECT 33
THE QUADRAFUZZ

The Quadrafuzz is a no-holds-barred distortion device that allows for a wide variety of different fuzz sounds—from smooth, liquid leads to chunky power chords that crash through a rhythm track. This is one fuzz that doesn't have either a "transistor" or a "tube" sound, but instead it seems to combine elements of the two and throws in its own personality on top of that.

What makes the Quadrafuzz different from other distortion devices is that it splits the guitar signal into four separate frequency bands (Lo, Mid 1, Mid 2, and Hi), distorts each band individually, and then sums the four bands to create a composite sound. This multiple fuzz approach offers several benefits:

- Chords and clusters of notes sound cleaner since there is less intermodulation distortion (that is, "harsh" distortion) than there would be with a single-channel fuzz.

- The filters can be carefully tuned to increase certain desirable characteristics of the overall guitar sound.

- Boosting individual frequency bands helps to increase the sustain at those parts of the audio spectrum.

These combined benefits result in a sound that is cleaner than that produced by a conventional fuzz and that also has more "character," due to the peaking action of the filters.

The Quadrafuzz includes far more than just distortion circuitry; it includes individual level controls for each channel, Hi/Lo filter resonance switches, tapped audio outputs for spreading the sound into stereo or quad (assuming you have a suitable mixer), a two-pole active low pass filter for precise overall tone shaping, an effects loop for adding other types of equalizers, CMOS electronic footswitching with an LED status indicator, low- or line-level operation, and consistent operation with supply voltages ranging from ±5 to ±20 volts DC. This is not an easy project to build—there are a lot of parts and wires—but I think you'll find your efforts amply rewarded. (This is also one project where I strongly recommend buying the parts kit from Paia Electronics, if for no other reason than for the ease of mounting components on the circuit board.)

HOW IT WORKS

While you don't have to understand the following theory behind the Quadrafuzz, the circuit demonstrates a lot of basic principles of musical electronics. So try to get through the schematic shown in Figs. 1 and 2 and pick up what you can; I hope you find it interesting and educational. Incidentally, Fig. 10-13 includes the input, output, tone control, and footswitch stages; Fig. 10-14 shows the four filter and distortion sections. Important

Fig. 10-13
Quadrafuzz input, output, tone control, and footswitch stages.

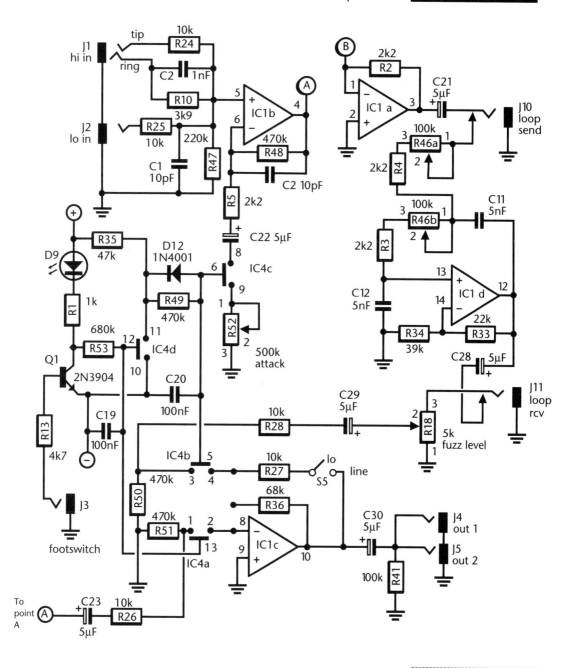

**Fig. 10-14
Quadrafuzz filter
and distortion
sections.**

note: the points labeled A and B on each schematic connect together.

The op amp labeled IC1b (integrated circuit 1b) is a preamp that accepts either a high-level input (via J1) or a low-level input (via J2). The Attack control (R52) sets IC1b's gain from a factor of 2 to 200. At higher attack settings, this stage introduces some

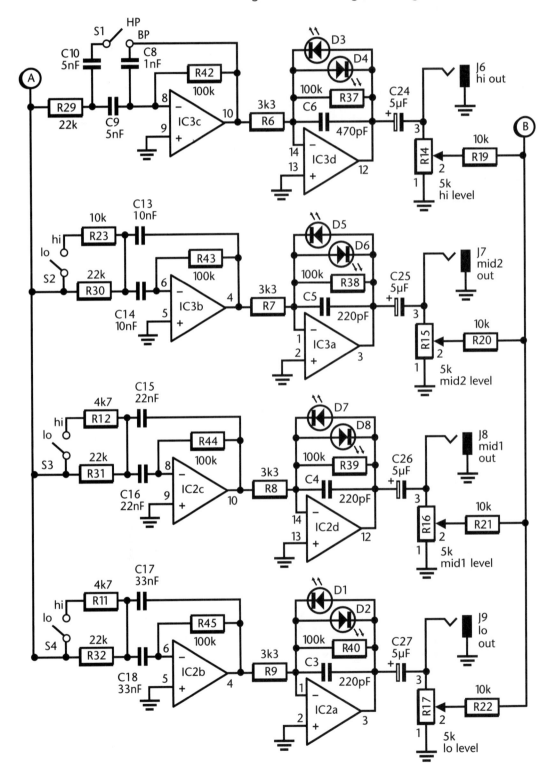

DO-IT-YOURSELF PROJECTS FOR GUITARISTS

broadband distortion of its own that is particularly useful for lead sounds.

The preamplified signal ends up at point A, then splits (via resistors R29-R32) into four bandpass filters. The filter built around IC2b (Lo) is tuned the lowest, the one built around IC2c (Mid 1) is tuned somewhat higher, and the filter built around IC3b (Mid 2) is tuned approximately one octave higher than Mid 1. The Hi filter, IC3c, is tuned one octave higher than Mid 2, but it also offers a switch-selectable bandpass or pseudo-high-pass response. The other filters include switches S2 through S4, which allow for increases in resonance (sharpness).

The filter outputs feed into individual distortion units built around IC2a, IC2d, IC3a, and IC3d. These stages use LEDs rather than the usual diodes as clipping (distortion-inducing) elements because they clip at a higher voltage, which allows for more output from each distortion stage. LEDs also seem to clip in a somewhat "gentler" fashion than regular diodes, thus giving what is probably best described as a more "rounded" sound.

Each filter output can be individually tapped (note that these outputs are in phase with the master output, so you won't run into cancellation problems if you use an external mixer to combine the individual outputs and the master output). Each filter also feeds its own level control, so you can regulate the balance of the various frequency bands. The level controls go to a mixer (IC1a), which combines the signals prior to feeding a tunable active filter (IC1d). This two-pole lowpass filter provides additional control over the final sound, and its characteristics seem very well suited to guitar—it almost sounds like a speaker emulator. Also note that the Loop Send jack (J10) and the Loop Receive jack (J11) bypass the filter, thus letting you patch other types of filters or signal processors in place of the Quadrafuzz filter, if desired.

The filter output proceeds to the Fuzz Level control, R18, which feeds the output mixer/electronic footswitch stage (IC1c and IC4a-IC4d). The four schematic symbols that look sort of like a pushbutton switch represent the individual switches inside a CMOS 4016 IC. These are arranged so that with the fuzz

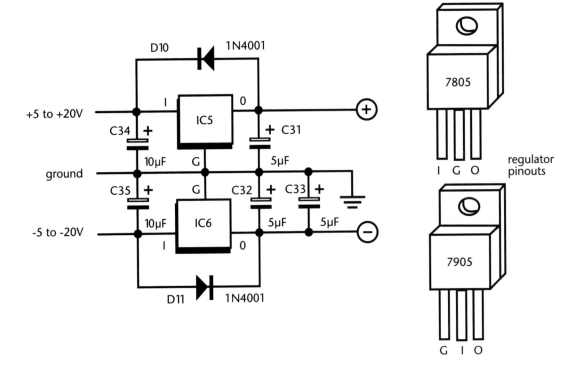

D10   1N4001

+5 to +20V

C34   +
10µF

ground

C35   +
10µF

-5 to -20V

I   IC5   0

G

C31
+   5µF

G

C32   +   C33   +
5µF   5µF

IC6

I   0

D11   1N4001

7805

regulator
pinouts

I   G   O

7905

G   I   O

**Fig. 10-15
Quadrafuzz power
regulators and
pinouts.**

bypassed, switch IC4c is open (thereby setting the preamp to minimum gain), and IC4a is closed (allowing the preamp output to feed into IC1c). When bypassed, IC4b is also open.

With the fuzz effect active, IC4c closes to provide for adjustment of IC1b's gain, IC4a opens to cut off the straight signal, and IC4b closes to let through the distorted signal. Diode D9, the status LED, is an integral part of the switching circuit. If for some reason you don't want to use an LED, then replace it with a 10k resistor.

Integrated circuits IC5 and IC6 in Fig. 10-15 are regulators that provide a stable power source to the Quadrafuzz. They accept a bipolar supply voltage in the range of ±5 to ±20 volts, and regulate it to a consistent ±5 volts DC. Diodes D10 and D11 provide protection if the regulators' outputs exceed their input voltages (a condition that could otherwise damage the chips).

So much for theory, now for practice.

CONSTRUCTION

The Quadrafuzz is a high-gain, low-level, high-input impedance device; it has just the right features to produce a growling mass of feedback and hum unless you wire things carefully. Since this is a relatively complex circuit, take careful note of the following cautions as you build the Quadrafuzz.

- You must use rosin-core solder and a low-wattage (no more than 40-60 watts) fine-tip soldering iron. Work slowly and carefully; pay close attention to the IC pin numbers, as well as the orientation of the diodes and electrolytic capacitors.

- Remember that R46 is a dual-ganged pot (two pots on one shaft).

- J1 is a stereo jack, but it is designed to accept a standard mono plug. Make sure that you wire up the tip and ring connections properly. (The reason for using a stereo jack is that plugging a standard mono plug into it creates some attenuation, and it also lowers the input impedance to a more suitable value for high-level signals.)

- Wiring layout is important. Keep the input and output leads physically separate from each other; if they must run close together (say, less than ½" apart), use shielded cable. In fact, for this particular project it's advisable to use shielded cable on all cable runs longer than a few inches, any cables that carry low-level signals, and cables that connect from the circuit board to outboard components. Granted, preparing shielded cable is a hassle—but it's a worthwhile hassle if you want the most stable and feedback-free operation.

  Incidentally, with any shielded cable used for this project, the shield should connect to the ground at one end only. In the parts kit for this project, the circuit board has a ground pad next to each signal pad for attaching the shield. If you make your own circuit board, it's a good idea to apply the same technique.

- Use sockets for all ICs.

- IC4 is a CMOS integrated circuit, and is therefore subject to damage from static electricity. Keep this IC in its conductive foam or aluminum carrier until you've finished wiring the entire unit, and then pop it into its socket right before testing. It's best to take this approach with the other ICs as well.

- For best results, use a good-quality power supply such as the one presented in this book. Do not connect the front panel to the circuit board ground point, but instead run a wire from J2's ground lug to the power supply ground (exception: if the power supply lines are long, connect J2's ground lug to the circuit board ground point instead). This should keep ground loop problems to a minimum.

- IC1-IC3 are given as 4136-type quad op amps. If these are hard to find in your area, you can substitute the TL074 or TL084, although these have a different pinout. You can also use six dual op amps instead, such as the NE5532.

- **Important:** Power supply connections are not shown for the various ICs in Fig. 10-13 and Fig. 10-14. If you're using the ICs given in the parts list, note that pin 11 of IC1, IC2, and IC3, as well as pin 14 of IC4, connect to the (+) power supply connection (see Fig. 1-16). Pin 7 of IC1, IC2, IC3, and IC4 connect to the (-) power supply connection. Also, the circled (+) and (-) in Fig. 10-13 similarly connect to the (+) and (-) power supply connections, respectively.

TESTING THE QUADRAFUZZ

Because the Quadrafuzz includes a fair amount of circuitry, it's possible for the thing to appear functional even if, for example, two of the filter sections are defective. Of course, the sound will be nowhere near as good under those conditions, so plan to spend some time testing the unit in order to make sure all is well before you get too involved in playing.

Plug your instrument into J2 (Lo In), and patch either J4 or J5 (Out) to your amp or monitoring system. Set the Lo/Line switch to match your amp's needs. The Quadrafuzz powers up in the bypassed position, so you will be hearing your straight guitar signal. Varying the unit's controls shouldn't affect the sound.

Now turn controls R14, R15, R16, R17, and R52 halfway up, R46 up full, R18 up about one-third of the way, make sure S1 is closed (BP position), and check that S2, S3, and S4 are open (low resonance position). Next plug a footswitch (or ¼" phone plug with its tip and ground shorted together) into J3. LED D9 should illuminate, and you should start hearing some fuzz effects. Adjust R18 for a good balance between distorted and straight sounds.

To check whether the filter and fuzz sections are working more or less properly, kick the Attack control full clockwise for maximum distortion, play a power chord, and look at LEDs D1 through D8. These should be glowing very faintly as you play (turn down the room lights to check). If not, there's a problem. It could be a burned out LED, bad connection, or whatever—but trace down the source of the trouble before continuing.

Now test the individual filters. Turn down R14, R15, R16, and R17; there should be no sound coming from the Quadrafuzz. Next turn each control up to get a feel for the different fuzz channel characteristics. The Lo channel will sound boomier, while the Hi channel will be thinner and more trebly. As you turn up each control, also flick the associated switch to observe the effect this makes on the sound. Each channel does not sound *radically* different from the others when listened to individually, but combining the channels makes for some very interesting effects. This is particularly true with the HP/BP switch. When listening to the Hi channel by itself, this switch appears to make very little difference.

Now vary the filter control and see how that changes the sound from bright to bassy. And if you want to experiment with the individual filter outputs or patch something into the effects loop to replace the Quadrafuzz lowpass filter, be my guest.

USING THE QUADRAFUZZ

After I had completed the final prototype and applied power, the Quadrafuzz didn't seem as good-sounding as I had remembered it during the breadboarding process. But within 15 minutes, I had rediscovered some of my favorite control settings and was getting the usual great sounds out of it. Moral of the story: it will take practice for you to learn this unit. Sure, this could have been designed as a preset device with a couple of killer sounds, but if you're going to build something this versatile, you deserve more. Your part of the deal is to learn the device well enough to focus on the cool sounds and avoid the duds.

Speaking of cool sounds, for heavy metal-type power chords try kicking the Attack control up full, turn up the Lo and Hi channels to the max, and leave Mid 1 and Mid 2 down (although adding a bit of Mid 1 sounds pretty good, too). The filter setting is also critical; I generally trim it back a tiny bit from full clockwise to keep the sound from getting too shrill. If you're into more of a chunky amp kind of sound, set the Attack knob up about halfway, Lo and Hi fully counterclockwise, and Mid 1 and Mid 2 fully clockwise. Also try the high resonance position for one or both of the mid channels.

For lead sounds, there are many possibilities. Of course, patching a compressor in front of the Quadrafuzz will increase sustain, but the inherent sustain is already quite good, providing that the Attack control is up full. Experiment with the various knobs, and try setting S1 to HP instead of BP from time to time.

I cannot emphasize enough that this is one device that must be *learned*. For example, there are four ways to control equalization when using the Quadrafuzz: via the Attack control (clockwise gives more highs), the individual filter channel and resonance controls, the lowpass filter frequency control, and of course, the tone controls on your guitar. These all interact to a certain extent and can all greatly influence the final sound. Practice!

TROUBLESHOOTING

Here are some possible problems you might run into when debugging the Quadrafuzz, along with suggested solutions.

- High-pitched whistling sound. First see if there could be a lead layout or shielding problem by pushing leads around. If separating certain leads solves or improves the problem, reroute the wires or use shielded cable instead. The problem could also be a control setting; compare the distorted and straight volume levels, and if necessary, turn down R18 to bring them into better balance. Setting R18 too high tends to promote feedback. Also try changing S1's setting from HP to BP, and turn down the Attack control if feedback problems persist.

- Fuzzed sound is present even when unit is bypassed. Check that the leads carrying high-level fuzz sounds do not pass by input leads or input coupling capacitors. Reroute wires, or push capacitors closer to the board.

- Overly harsh distortion on one channel. One of the LEDs is probably either burned out from excess heat during soldering or improperly oriented.

If you do run into problems, don't be discouraged. When working properly, this is a really great-sounding device. I hope you find it as useful an addition to your collection of effects as I have.

PARTS LIST

Resistors   (1/4 watt, 5% tolerance, except as noted)

R1	1k
R2-R5	2.2k (2k2)
R6-R9	3.3k (3k3)
R10	3.9k (3k9)
R11-R13	4.7k (4k7)
R14-R18	5k audio or linear taper potentiometer
R19-R28	10k
R29-R33	22k
R34	39k
R35	47k
R36	68k
R37-R45	100k
R46a/R46b	100k dual ganged linear taper potentiometer
R47	220k
R48-R51	470k
R52	500k linear taper potentiometer
R53	680k

PARTS LIST *(continued)*

Capacitors (10 working volts or greater, except as indicated)

C1, C2	10pF disc ceramic
C3-C5	220pF disc ceramic
C6	470pF disc ceramic
C7, C8	0.001µF (1nF) disc ceramic or polystyrene

(C9-C18 should be mylar, polystyrene, or other precision capacitors for best results)

C9-C12	0.005µF (5nF)
C13, C14	0.01µF (10nF)
C15, C16	0.022uF (22nF)
C17, C18	0.033µF (33nF)
C19, C20	0.1µF (100nF)
C21-C33	5µF electrolytic or tantalum
C34, C35	10µF/25 working volts electrolytic or tantalum

Semiconductors

D1-D9	Red LED
D10-D12	1N4001 or equivalent diode
IC1-IC3	RC4136, XR4136, or equivalent quad op amp (see text)
IC4	CD4016 CMOS quad switch
IC5	7805 +5V regulator
IC6	7905 -5V regulator
Q1	2N3904 NPN general purpose transistor

Other parts

S1-S5	SPST or SPDT switches
J1	Stereo, open circuit, ¼" phone jack
J2-J9	Mono, open circuit, ¼" phone jacks
J10, J11	Mono, closed circuit, ¼" phone jacks
Misc.	Circuit board, knobs, wire, front panel, etc.

✳ PROJECT 34
THE ROCKTAVE DIVIDER

It's not a fancy, expensive digital pitch transposer—but it does give vintage octave divider sounds without the tracking problems and sonic limitations of older models.

The Rocktave Divider not only does what traditional octave dividers do, but has a few other tricks up its sleeve as well, such as:

- **Multiple sounds.** You can mix any proportion of octave lower sound (divide by 2), two octaves lower sound (divide by 4), or normal distortion sound (fundamental) along with the straight sound.

- **Sustain-plus-decay dynamics.** All of the above sounds have a sustained, compressed character until your string hits its final stages of decay. Then, as the string fades out, the level of the divided and/or fuzzed sounds tracks your instrument's dynamics for a more interesting, life like sound.

- **No "sputtering" at the end of notes.** Octave dividers cannot track extremely weak signals, so as a note fades out, simple octave boxes tend to produce an annoying, sputtering kind of effect. However, the dynamics-generating part of this circuit is designed so that the divided signal decays at a slightly faster rate than the note which you're playing. Thus, the divided signal disappears just before the point at which sputtering would normally occur.

- **Tone control.** When pulled back all the way (minimum treble), you can get Wes Montgomery-like sounds which are mellow and, thanks to the decay dynamics, extremely natural-sounding. But set the tone to 10, and you'll get a raspy, fuzzy, sustained sound which is about as rock-and-roll as you're going to get.

- **Good tracking.** I won't claim that a circuit this basic is perfect, but it does work extremely well (of course, like other simple octave dividers, the Rocktave Divider tracks only single notes, not chords). In fact, if you use your bass pickup, and remember to pick lightly below the fifth fret or so, you'll have good to excellent tracking over the entire range of the neck. Above the fifth fret, you can get pretty wild and the thing will still track well (although at the very highest notes you may have to hit the strings a little harder than usual). For those with a lighter- or heavier-than-average touch, later on we'll describe how to customize the Rocktave Divider to make the best possible match with your playing style.

- **Simple power requirements.** The Rocktave Divider works off as little as 6.5V to as much as 12V DC, so a 9V transistor radio battery makes a good power source. Power requirements are less than 10 mA (typically about 7 mA or so).

HOW IT WORKS

Referring to the schematic (Fig. 10-16), J1 is the input jack. It also doubles as an on/off switch because when you plug a standard mono cord into this stereo jack, the connection marked "tip" contacts the tip of the plug and the connection marked "ring" contacts the sleeve (ground), thus providing a path for the battery's (-) end to ground through the ring connection. For longest battery life, always unplug the input cord after you've finished playing.

IC1b amplifies and buffers your signal. This signal goes to two places: the output mixer (IC1c), which mixes this straight signal in with the divided sounds, and to IC1a. IC1a amplifies your signal a bit more to provide the best match for the compressor built around IC2a.

IC2a is half of a 571 or 570 compander chip. It's set up so that C4 provides lots of low pass filtering, which emphasizes the fundamental and reduces the harmonic content to minimize "octave skipping" and other tracking problems. Using both filtering and compression produces a smooth, consistent signal which is easier to divide down than a straight guitar signal.

After being conditioned, the guitar signal hits IC1d. This is a comparator with a self-adjusting threshold; the self-adjusting feature means that you get maximum possible sustain out of this

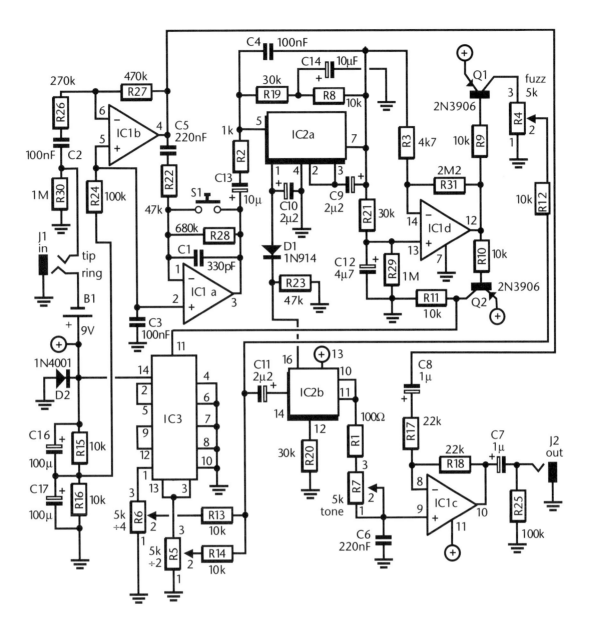

stage. IC1d then feeds two transistors. Q1 produces a square wave whose frequency equals that of the note you're playing on the guitar. R4 taps this square wave, and sends it to expander IC2b prior to going to the output mixer. Q2 acts in a similar fashion to Q1. It conditions the signal coming out of IC1d and drives the actual octave dividers, which are part of IC3.

IC3 is a CMOS dual flip-flop, where both stages are set up to divide by 2. Thus, one flip-flop's output is a square wave one octave below your guitar signal (tapped by R5), and the other flip-flop's output is a square wave two octaves below your guitar signal (tapped by R6). These two outputs, along with the output tapped by R4, mix together through R12-R14 and feed IC2b.

Fig. 10-16
Rocktave Divider schematic.

IC2b is set up as an expander, but we've done something a little unusual here. By tying pin 16 to pin 1, the dynamics of this stage follow the dynamics of IC2a, which in turn follows the dynamics of your guitar note. D1 reduces the voltage going to IC2b somewhat, which is why the divided note always decays just a little bit before your straight signal. IC2b's output feeds tone control R7, which enters output mixer IC1c via pin 9. In the meantime, the straight signal goes into IC1c via pin 8. IC1c's output couples through C7 to J2, the output jack.

Now for a few fine points. Note that all points marked with a circled (+) connect together; this is the 9V supply point. The Rock-tave Divider also requires a 4.5V supply, provided by the voltage divider made up of R15 and R16. This point connects to R24.

S1 is the bypass switch. With S1 open, the octave divider works normally, with the straight signal and divided signals appearing at IC1c's output. With S1 closed, IC1a essentially "turns off," thus leaving only the straight signal present at the output. Simple, yes… but it works and provides a noiseless switching action.

FINDING PARTS

All parts are pretty common, with the possible exception of the 570 and 4136. These are often available from mail-order houses that advertise in the back of electronics magazines; a complete kit of parts is available from Paia Electronics.

If desired, you can substitute the more common TL074 or TL084 quad op amp for the 4136, although the pinout will be different compared to the schematic. Or, you can substitute two dual op amps, such as the NE5532.

CONSTRUCTION TIPS

All the standard cautions apply: observe the polarity of electrolytic capacitors and diodes (very important), use sockets for all ICs, heat sink the transistor leads (by clipping an alligator clip to the lead) when soldering to minimize the possibility of heat damage, and make sure you use a fresh battery when testing. Also, IC3 is a CMOS IC which may be destroyed by static electricity discharges. Keep this part in its conductive foam or foil until construction is complete, then, while holding the circuit board ground with one hand, use your other hand to pop the IC into its socket.

USING THE ROCKTAVE DIVIDER

Patch your guitar into J1, patch J2 to your amp, and you should be ready to kick into action. Select the bass (rhythm/neck) pickup for best results, and pick *cleanly*—if more than one string is vibrating at a time, the sound will be inconsistent. In most cases, you may leave the tone control at the full treble position, but if you have octave skipping problems, turn the tone control down. Start playing around the middle of the neck to familiarize yourself with the way the box tracks, and experiment with the various controls. Remember to pick more softly as you hit the lower end of the neck. Don't expect instant perfection, since octave dividers require practice for best results. After about half an hour, though, you should have the box pretty well figured out.

For a fuzz-with-dynamics sound, turn the tone control clockwise (full treble), turn up R4, and turn down R5 and R6. This sound resembles the Ultra-Fuzz (project #6 in the book *Electronic Projects for Musicians),* but with added dynamics. For a Wes Montgomery type of effect, turn the tone control full back for the bassiest sound, turn up R5, and turn down R4 and R6. Thanks to the dynamics and muted sound, the sound is quite warm and natural—not at all electronic sounding.

For a thick, monster rock lead sound, turn up the tone control, turn up R4, and turn up R5 and R6 to suit. You'll be amazed at the fullness of the sound. Adding a little equalization or chorusing makes the sound even bigger.

One caution: If you turn up R4, R5, and R6 close to maximum, the signals going through them might overload IC2b. This will make the dynamics circuitry behave improperly, and may produce ugly distorted sounds. Should these problems occur, trim back a bit on these controls.

CUSTOMIZATION

There are numerous changes you can make to the Rocktave Divider. First, we'll discuss those that relate to playing style.

The Rocktave Divider is intended to be compatible with the vast majority of guitars and playing styles. However, there are always those players with a very soft "touch" (or have guitars with weak pickups), and those who hit their strings as if they were mortal enemies. The symptoms of too soft a touch are inadequate divided level and poor sustain. If you experience these problems, increase C5 to 1μF and decrease R22 to 22k (if that doesn't make enough of a difference, try 10k). If you play too hard, chances are the tracking will be erratic, and the dynamics circuitry will not work correctly (and you could get "sputtering" on the ends of notes as well). The cure is simple: increase the value of R22 to 100k, 150k, or if you have plutonium pickups and a bionic hand, then maybe even 220k will be necessary.

Here are some other possible modifications:

- **Unity gain through the effect.** This box is set up to give a bit of boost at the output. If you don't want this, change R17 to 39k.

- **+15V operation.** Change R19 to 68k and increase R12 through R14 to about 22k.

- **Greater overall output.** Increase R18.

- **Jazz tone only.** If you're not much into rock and roll fuzz sounds, change C6 to 1μF.

- **Stereo processing.** Fig. 10-17 shows how to insert three additional components (stereo closed circuit ¼" jack and two 5μF electrolytic capacitors) between C8 and R17 to add a direct output to the Rocktave Divider. This output carries the straight sound; the divided and fuzzed sounds, less any straight sound, appear at J2. You can pan this output and the direct output to opposite ends of the stereo field, plug them into two channels of a two channel amp, or add processing to the divided sound present at J2 without affecting the straight signal.

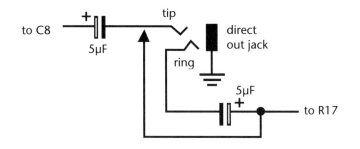

Fig. 10-17
Adding a direct output to the Rocktave Divider.

PARTS LIST

Resistors (1/4 watt, 5% or 10% tolerance unless otherwise noted)

R1	100Ω
R2	1k
R3	4.7k (4k7)
R4-R7	5k potentiometer
R8-R16	10k
R17, R18	22k
R19-R21	30k (5%)
R22, R23	47k
R24, R25	100k
R26	270k
R27	470k
R28	680k
R29, R30	1M
R31	2.2M (2M2)

Capacitors (16V or greater working voltage)

C1	330pF polystyrene
C2, C3	0.1µF (100nF) disc or mylar
C4	0.1µF (100nF) mylar
C5, C6	0.22µF (220nF) mylar
C7, C8	1µF electrolytic
C9-C11	2.2µF (2µ2) electrolytic
C12	4.7µF (4µ7) electrolytic
C13, C14	10µF electrolytic
C15, C16	100µF electrolytic

Semiconductors

D1	1N914 or equivalent
D2	1N4001 or equivalent
IC1	RC4136 or XR4136 quad op amp (see text)
IC2	NE571 or NE570 compander

PARTS LIST *(continued)*

IC3	CD4013 dual flip-flop
Q1, Q2	2N3906 PNP general purpose transistor

Other parts

J1	Stereo, open circuit, ¼" phone jack
J2	Mono, open circuit, ¼" phone jack
S1	SPST push-on/push-off footswitch
Misc.	Case, circuit board, knobs, wire, solder, etc.

MORE ROCKTAVE DIVISIONS

If you're willing to give up the stock divide-by-4 output, you can modify the Rocktave Divider to divide the guitar signal by either 2, 3, 4, 5, 6, 7, 8, 9, 10, or 11. Not all of these divisions are real useful musically; here's a list of what notes are produced for the various divisors, assuming an "E" input note.

2	E one octave below
3	A below the above E
4	E two octaves below
5	C below the above E
6	A below the above C
7	Between F# and G below the above A
8	E three octaves below
9	D below the above E
10	C below the above D
11	Between A# and B below the above C

Of these, divide by 2 through 6 are the most useful musically. However, for special effects the other outputs have their uses as well.

HOW IT WORKS

The schematic (Fig. 10-18) shows the complete mod. The CD4017 is a *decade counter/divider,* which can divide an input square wave by 2 through 11, depending on which pin connects to the reset input (pin 15). For example, jumpering pin 1 to pin 15 gives divide-by-5, jumpering pin 4 to pin 15 gives divide-by-2, pin 5 to pin 15 gives divide-by-6, and so on according to the divisor numbers given on the left-hand side of the schematic. I'd suggest using a rotary switch to switch between the divisors you want to use. As one example, if you have a five-position switch you could select between divide by 3, 4, 5, 6, and 9.

THE MODIFICATION

Use a 16-pin socket for the 4017, and make all connections to this socket. For best results, wire the socket and two resistors to a piece of perf board or circuit board, make the connections listed below to the Rocktave divider, and insulate the mod circuit board with some tape so that it doesn't short out to the other circuitry. Remember too that the 4017 is a CMOS integrated circuit, so follow the precautions given earlier under "Construction Tips" to prevent static electricity damage.

If you don't want to drill any additional holes in the case, simply jumper pin 15 to pin 7. This provides the divide-by-3 function, which is probably the most musically valid option. Otherwise, wire up a switch to connect pin 15 to the desired divisor pins. For example, with an SPDT switch you might want to choose between divide-by-3 (pin 7) and divide-by-4 (pin 10).

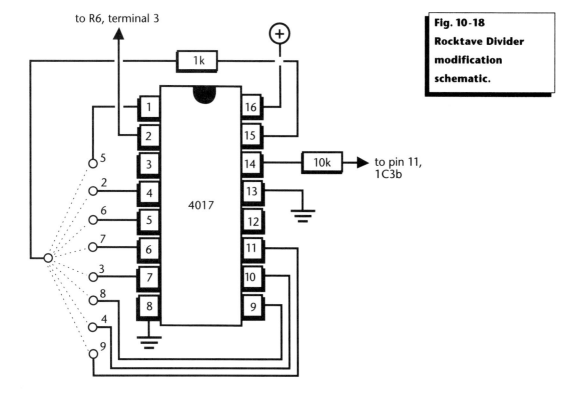

Fig. 10-18 Rocktave Divider modification schematic.

Connect a wire to pin 11 of IC3b (note that if you bought the parts kit, there is a wire jumper next to pin 11 to which you can solder this lead), and connect the other end of this wire through a 10k resistor to pin 14 of the 4017. Next, disconnect the lead going from IC3 pin 1 to terminal 3 of R6. This disables the stock divide-by-four output. Connect a wire from pin 2 of the 4017 to terminal 3 of R6. This lets R6 control the level of the divided signal coming from the 4017.

Finally, connect the 4017's two ground connections to the Rocktave Divider ground, and connect pin 16 from the 4017 to the Rocktave Divider's positive supply.

TESTING

This is the fun part. Turn up R6, and you'll hear your new divided sound. With divide-by-3, the effect resembles the parallel harmony effects you'd get with a guitar synthesizer, and this can really thicken up your sound. Check it out!

BONUS MOD

Here's another mod which is extremely easy yet produces some wild timbres. The tradeoff is that the dynamics don't track as well (which gives more noise at the end of notes), but this effect is so nasty you won't care about any residual noise. Simply connect a 0.1µF (100nF) capacitor between pin 16 and pin 2 of IC2. This super-distorts the compander chip to give brassy, fat, buzz-saw sounds.

✴ PROJECT 35
"STACK IN A BOX" TUBE PREAMP

If you've been lusting after the sound of a tube preamp but can't swing the price of admission, Stack in a Box (SIAB) delivers superior tube sound without busting your budget.

The Stack in a Box is no stripped-down piece of gear: there's a clean preamp stage, high and low impedance unbalanced inputs, two different speaker simulator settings, bright and "fat" switches, effects loop, balanced XLR output for interfacing with pro studio gear, and standard unbalanced ¼" phone outputs …and the sound is *way* cool.

HOW IT WORKS

SIAB (Fig. 10-19) combines solid-state and tube circuitry. Preamp IC1a provides clean gain (up to 10X, set by the Crunch control) to overload the first tube stage. This in turn feeds effects loop J1 and J2. To avoid compromising the sound, the effect should have a high input impedance (greater than 100k). The signal goes to the second tube stage via Drive control R17, which adjusts the waveform symmetry and amount of distortion.

Next comes the speaker simulator, a 5-pole filter built around IC1b and IC2a, that mimics the high-frequency rolloff of a typical cabinet with 12" speakers. S4 chooses between the full simulator (Sim 2) and a brighter, buzzier version (Sim 1). Fat switch S2 affects the lows; Bright switch S3 alters the highs. When using SIAB to feed an amp that drives a guitar speaker cabinet, you can bypass the speaker simulator with S1 (note that the Bright switch is still active).

Output control R23 sets the overall level and feeds the non-inverting output (J5) as well as a stage that inverts the phase to provide an inverted output (J6). J7 is a balanced XLR female connector for direct connection to studio consoles; for compatibility with balanced gear that does not follow the IEC standard for XLR pin polarity, S5 chooses whether pin 2 or 3 is "hot."

Tubes require higher voltages than solid state gear, so this implies a high-voltage transformer that can be both expensive and potentially hazardous. IC3 and D3-D7 provide a voltage multiplying circuit that allows the use of a 12V transformer yet still provides 42 volts to power the tube plates.

FINDING PARTS/CONSTRUCTION

This is not a project for novices; practice on some simple projects first—electronic circuits can be hazardous! It is beyond the scope

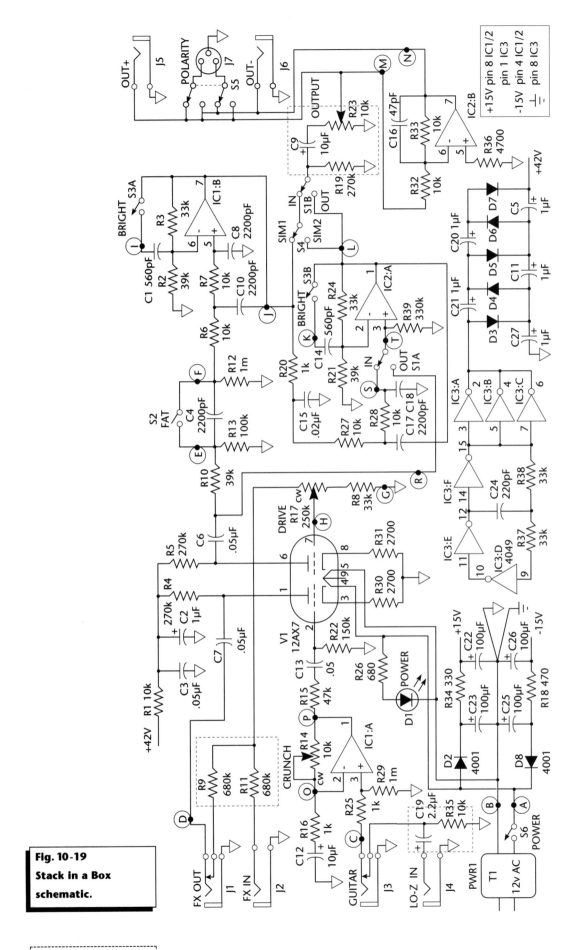

Fig. 10-19
Stack in a Box
schematic.

of this book to provide full details on electronic construction, so if you have any doubts about your abilities, find someone with suitable experience who can help.

Most parts are available from mail-order electronics companies. In addition, a kit of parts is available from Paia Electronics. Due to the complexity of the circuit and possibilities for error, I recommend the parts kit (which has step-by-step instructions) unless you are an experienced constructor.

The off-board parts hook into the circuit board at the points indicated with letters on the schematic. Use shielded cables on the high impedance connections (C, D, E, H, and R), and keep all wires as short and direct as possible. The power supply can generate electrical noise; the rear view photo shows how to mount a metal shield, fashioned out of sheet aluminum, so that it "floats" above the circuit board components.

USING THE STACK IN A BOX

With your amp volume turned down, plug your guitar into jack J3 (or connect a low impedance source, such as a synth output, into J4). ¼" unbalanced amp or mixer inputs should hook into J5 (non-inverting out), and XLR balanced inputs should patch into J7. To feed ¼" stereo jack balanced inputs, make up a cord that connects the inverted out to a stereo plug's ring connection, the non-inverted out to the tip connection, and the ground for both outputs to the plug ground.

Turn on power and let the tube warm up. If all is well, start fiddling with the dials. If you detect strange odors, smoke, buzzes, sparks, or other possible problems, shut down power *immediately* and look over your wiring for errors.

There are some "sweet spot" control combinations, so don't be discouraged if the SIAB doesn't sound great the second you plug it in—it takes a little experimentation to match the various controls to your setup. Watch out for:

■ The Crunch control provides clean gain for overloading the tube and creating more distortion. Too much crunch with high-level inputs could overload the input preamp, creating solid-state distortion. This will contribute an ugly buzzing sound on top of the smooth tube distortion.

■ Start with the Drive control up halfway. This affects the waveform symmetry; rotating Drive more clockwise adds a subtle attack or edge to the sound, while counterclockwise gives a mellower tone.

■ If you're plugging into a guitar amp, turn the speaker simulator off. When plugging into a mixer, set the speaker simulator in/out switch to in, simulator to Sim 2, bright to off, and fat to on. Experiment with different simulator, bright, and fat settings to see which combination works best for you.

■ The SIAB can produce substantial gain, so don't turn up the output control so much that it overloads subsequent stages (unless, of course, that's the effect you want).

And that's about all there is to it. If you're working in the studio, try the SIAB with other sound sources—it can really warm up the sound of synthesizers, drum machines, and even vocals.

Acknowledgement: A big thanks to John Simonton, who not only co-designed the circuit (and deserves particular credit for the clever power supply trick), but also wrote the section below on why the SIAB sounds so good.

WHY DOES THE STACK IN A BOX SOUND SO GOOD?

All amplifiers distort if you drive them hard enough, but tubes and transistors distort differently. Engineers use transfer curves to show the relationship of an amplifier's output signal to its input. The input (coming in from the bottom) "reflects" off the curve to produce the output at the right.

Fig. 10-20A, a transistor amp transfer curve, shows that everything is linear until you suddenly run out of headroom, at which point the signal clips. This drastic clipping produces high amplitude harmonics.

Fig. 10-20B, a tube transfer curve, is linear only for small signals. The ends of the curve, which bend over gradually rather

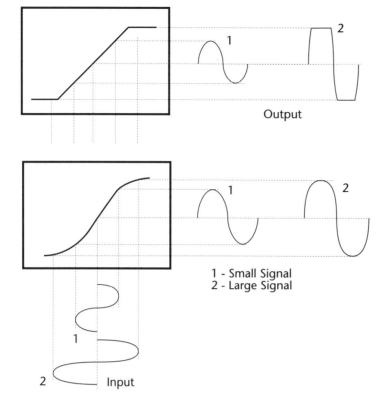

a) Solid State
"Clipping" produces
higher order, higher
amplitude harmonics.

b) Tube Amp
"Squashing" produces
lower order harmonics
with smaller amplitudes.

1 - Small Signal
2 - Large Signal

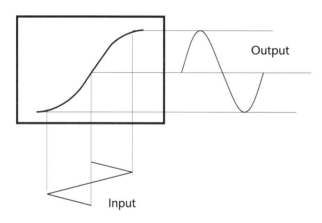

Output

Input

Fig. 10-20
Tube transfer
function.

than suddenly reach a plateau, "squash" the signal rather than clip it at higher levels. This produces a more rounded waveform, and results in much of the characteristic "tube sound."

The SIAB exaggerates the naturally soft curve common to all tubes to come up with almost a caricature of a tube amp. Running the tube at low supply voltage and plate current puts it way down in the non-linear region of its operating range (a region generally considered so uninteresting it doesn't even show up in reference books—but it's fine for guitar preamps). The two cascaded tube stages complement one another; one rounds the upper end of the transfer curve and other the bottom, providing a symmetrical transfer curve. Altering the drive control changes the symmetry.

PARTS LIST

Resistors	(1/4 watt except as noted)
R1	10k
R2,21	39k
R3,24	33k
R4, 5, 19	270k
R6, 7, 27, 28, 32, 33	10k
R8, 37, 38	33k
R9, 11	680k
R10	39k
R12, 29	1M
R13	100k
R14	10k pot (Crunch)
R15	47k
R16, 20, 25	1k
R17	250k pot (Drive)
R18, 34	470Ω
R22	150k
R23	10k pot (Output)
R26	680Ω
R30, 31	2.7k (2k7)
R35	10k
R36	4.7k (4k7)

Capacitors (Those marked with * should be polystyrene or mylar. All capacitors should be 50 or more working volts)

C1, 14	560pF*
C2, 5, 11, 20, 21, 27	1µF
C3, 6, 7, 13	0.05µF (50nF)
C4, 8, 10, 17, 18	2200pF (2n2)*
C9, 12	10µF
C15	0.022µF (22nF)
C16	47pF
C19	2.2µF (2µ2)

C22, 23, 25, 26	100µF
C24	220pF

Semiconductors/Tubes

D1	Visible LED
D2-8	1N4001 power diode
IC1, 2	NE5532 dual op amp
IC3	CD4049 hex CMOS inverter
V1	12AX7 dual triode

Other parts

J1, 3	Mono, closed circuit, ¼" phone jack
J2, 4-6	Mono, open circuit, ¼" phone jack
J7	Male XLR connector
S1	DPDT switch (simulator bypass)
S2	SPST switch (fat option)
S3	DPST switch (bright option)
S4	SPDT switch (simulator select)
S5	DPDT switch (XLR out polarity)
S6	SPST switch (power)
T1	12 VAC wall transformer, 500 mA or greater
Misc.	Tube and IC sockets, circuit board, front panel, knobs, wire, solder, etc.